BEING A WIDOW

BEING A WIDOW

LYNN CAINE

G.K.HALL &CO.
Boston, Massachusetts
1990

Published in Large Print by arrangement with
William Morrow and Company, Inc.

G.K. Hall Large Print Book Series.

Set in 18 pt. Plantin.

Library of Congress Cataloging in Publication Data

Caine, Lynn.
  Being a widow / Lynn Caine.
       p.   cm—(G.K. Hall large print book series)
    ISBN 0-8161-4792-2
    1. Widows—United States—Life skills guides.   2. Widows—United
States—Psychology.   3. Large type books.   I.Title.
  [HQ1058.5.U5C34   1990b]
  306.88—dc20   89–24524

TO ELIZABETH AND JON, AGAIN

CONTENTS

AUTHOR'S FOREWORD

I've always thought that it is extremely unfair that we have only one life, since we need at least two: one for practice—like a dress rehearsal—and one for the real thing.

Given another chance, I would know exactly what to do—and exactly what not to do—in the most critical period of my life. This period began when my husband's doctor—his closest friend since boyhood—diagnosed the cancer of the liver from which my husband, Martin, would die fourteen months later.

In my impeccable ignorance of death and dying, I did everything wrong. Unfortunately, I'll never have the chance to make it up to my husband, my children, or myself. What I can do is share my experience and the experience of other widows in the hope that I can help make people more aware of the consequences of ignorance.

The first thing I would change about my reaction to Martin's illness is that I would be a lot less heroic and a lot more realistic. Martin and I knew from the beginning that his prognosis was zero. And what did we do? We playacted, assuming roles we considered admirable and playing to the hilt the gallant young couple facing death with courage, honesty, and grace under pressure. It was a great act, and we fooled a lot of people. We even fooled ourselves—for a while.

Had I been more open about my emotions, I might have helped Martin to be more open about his. As it was, we were both locked into our feelings and alienated from each other. What is clear to me now is that though we were able to share life, we were unable to share death.

The life that we had together—we were married for seventeen years—was a charmed one, and we felt blessed. Martin had his flourishing law practice, and I had my publicity job in publishing. We were even more blessed with our children—Jonathan and Elizabeth, or Buffy, as she's known. Our lives were filled with good friends, good music, and laughter. I thought it would last forever.

Martin was a war hero. He had been seriously wounded in World War II when his plane was shot down on a return raid from oil fields in Ploesti, Romania. He had shrapnel in his head and almost lost a leg. Martin returned from the war with a Silver Star awarded for gallantry in action, and a 90-percent medical-disability rating.

I didn't think too much about his medical history, though I knew that his disability rating made him eligible for a lifetime pension, but ineligible for commercial life insurance. Why did I need to think about that? We were young, and we both had good jobs and made enough money. Grown-up matters like illness were something that only concerned old people. As for death, I didn't think about that at all.

But then it happened. Martin died. I was left a widow with no insurance, no savings, a low-paying job, debts, and two small children. My nightmare began.

I write about these days in my first book, *Widow*. It is, in part, the story of how much my ignorance cost me. And that is another thing I would change about how I dealt with Martin's death. I would not be ignorant. I would read about death just as I've read about cooking or pregnancy or art. I would educate myself if I had it to do over again.

The popularity of *Widow* catapulted me into a fifteen-year odyssey of lectures, seminars, book-promotion tours, and television and radio appearances that has taken me back and forth across the United States and Canada. It brought me into contact with thousands of widows who found themselves in the same situation I was in. We talked, and I learned a lot from them and from their letters, too—letters thanking me for writing honestly about what happened in my life and letters sharing their own experiences of widowhood. I was overwhelmed with the outpouring of loving gratitude I received. And from a never-ending round of lectures, workshops, interviews I learned that I am not alone with my problems and, more importantly, how grateful other widows are to know that *they* are not alone.

The quotes in this book are representative of the many telephone calls I still get daily from widows and the meetings and seminars I've hosted. In truth, the book was written to answer questions I'm commonly asked. These years of meeting and communicating with other widows have given me insight and comfort and have produced the body of knowledge I want to share in this book.

I had no idea that such a powerful stream of communication would result from *Widow* and the other books I've written. It still amazes me a little to receive the morning mail and open a letter that begins, "Dear Lynn, I don't usually write to strangers, but I've been a widow for six months, and I am still so afraid. I can't eat. I can't sleep. Will I ever get through this? . . ." Some of the most difficult letters and phone calls have been about children. Widows tell me that their children cry all the time or that they can't cry at all, that they isolate themselves, that they're terrified of being abandoned by the remaining parent. I would be a lot more helpful to my children if I had it to do over again.

At seminars and workshops, so many widows shared with me their feelings of loneliness; their need for companionship, love, and sex in their lives—and their total frustration with not knowing how to enter the frightening sexual arena. As one widow put it, "It sounds like a bad joke, but there are things I want to do in bed other than read." No one has to be alone. There are many things a widow can do to have a social life and love life again. One thing that helps is knowing how a lot of other women have faced the emergence of sexuality, and that's one of the reasons for this book. We're really not alone, and we can learn from each other.

And then there's the question, "Who am I now?" No longer half of a couple, how can I face ridiculous questions and really insulting advice from well-meaning friends like "How much money did he leave you?" and "You really should sell that big house." You can deal effectively with this, and I learned it the hard way. Now I can teach how to become an assertive widow and how to express feelings constructively—and in a way that won't alienate friends. I want to pass this along, too, for one deeply felt reason.

This is the book I wish I had been able to turn to when Martin died! Writing it is the only way I know of saying thank you for all the sharing.

—Lynn Caine
New York, 1987

ACKNOWLEDGMENTS

I am grateful to the many widows who have generously given me the benefit of their experiences. Their contributions are the foundation of this book.

My thanks to Anne Rosberger of the Bereavement and Loss Center of New York, and to Sister Catherine Seeley and Colleen Scanlon of Calvary Hospital, and to the many other medical professionals who gave advice and support to this project.

My deep thanks to my friend and editor, Eleanor Friede, for understanding the concept of this book, and very special thanks to Barbara Bowen for making it all a reality.

BEING A WIDOW

THE IMPACT OF DEATH

"Mrs. Caine," said the voice on the other end of the phone, "your husband died this morning."

I was sitting up in bed. It was late morning on a gray and rainy Thursday, and I was home from work with what turned out later to be viral pneumonia. My nine-year-old son, Jon, was with me. He'd been sent home from school after throwing up on his science project. I couldn't have planned a more perfect day for our living nightmare to begin to really take form. It was miserable even without the news.

"Your husband died this morning." That's exactly what the doctor said. There wasn't a need to say anything more. Martin had been in a coma for thirteen days, after spending fourteen months slowly dying of cancer. I had been regularly traveling back and forth between New York and the hospital in Baltimore, until one of the doctors told me there

wasn't any point. It was a week or so before he died, and Martin was so drugged he didn't even know I was there. "You have two young children, and there's nothing more you can do here," said the doctor. "Go home." So I went home to wait for the call. There were times when I looked forward to it, even prayed for it. I wanted Martin to live, but I wanted *it* to be over. Funny, but I can't remember anything beyond those five words. I don't remember what I said, what I did, or whom I called—nothing. Some years later I asked my son, Jon, to fill me in. "Did I cry?" I wondered. "No," he said. "You were acting brave."

I had watched Martin—a strong, tall, handsome man of fifty—deteriorate, until he became someone I hardly recognized as my husband, and still I pretended he wasn't going to die. Jon's telling me that I acted brave really said it. That's something Martin and I did very well together. From the first diagnosis, we set up a fantasy life that had nothing to do with what was really happening. Martin was sure that he would be the seventh patient in the world to beat liver cancer. We never shared our feelings, our fears, or our love in any way that connected us to the reality of his prognosis. The truth

2

is that we were afraid to face it and too uninformed to know how damaging that was.

Some unknown force propelled me through the days and weeks following Martin's death. I know now that it's called shock. Most widows describe their feelings during this time as "I walked around like a robot"; "It was as though I was living in a thick fog"; or "I felt like I had been given shock treatment, and it left me dazed and unsure of where I was." A friend of mine told me that she felt like her head was not connected to her body. My own feeling is that the initial impact of death is so overwhelming that some kind of natural shutdown occurs. Maybe it's a built-in way we have of protecting ourselves so that we can do what needs to be done in those early days. You can do lots of things when you're in shock. I arranged a cremation, a memorial service, and a large party. As I wrote in *Widow*, handling the cremation and the storage of Martin's ashes was no more emotional for me than phoning in a grocery order. It's true, I was cool, controlled, and very brave. Actually I was numb, so numb that I was unaware that I was in pain. I was like the injured car-accident victim who gets up and walks away from a bloody crash saying,

3

"Who, me? Hurt? I feel fine." Eventually, it all caught up with me, and it hurt like hell.

That was nearly twenty years ago, and during that time much has changed about the way we deal with death. The biggest change is that we recognize the need to deal with it at all. When I was newly widowed, terms like "anticipatory grief" and "obsessive reminiscence," weren't thrown around by people like you and me. At least I never heard them. For fourteen months, I had been experiencing a form of anticipatory grief, and I didn't even know it. But mine was unguided, uneducated grief, and therein lies the big difference.

> We should have wept and talked together about death, but I smiled, was cheerful, and talked of getting well, even though I knew it was a lost war.

THE STAGES OF WIDOWHOOD

There has been a quiet movement going on over the last ten years or so. I say quiet because it's not the kind of thing you hear much about on the evening news, although we do more now because of AIDS and the increasing number of hospices that have been established to help the dying. The movement might be called understanding death, or bereavement counseling, or grief awareness. It means that today there is a network of helpers available who acknowledge not only the needs of the dying, but those of the survivor as well. There are more individual counselors who have better training in and understanding of the bereavement process. Medical professionals don't pigeonhole all the circumstances of death and the ages and backgrounds of widows in the same way anymore, and they don't approach grief with isolated step-by-step, stage-by-stage guidelines. They acknowledge that it just isn't the neat little package it was originally thought to be.

My first book, *Widow*, tells, in detail, each stage of widowhood as *I* experienced it. I can run down the basic list for you: numbness, shock, denial, anger, disorientation, depression, guilt, panic, and acceptance. Even though many studies done in the United States and England tell us that these stages of grief are predictable, every widow's personal journey through them is unique. That is a relatively new idea in bereavement counseling. I can't tell you—and neither can anyone else—when you'll feel any of these

5

emotions and face these problems or how long they'll last. Each woman responds to the death of her husband in her own way. The stages of grief can overlap or be jumbled together, or they can show up in an order different from the way they are presented here. There is no such thing as normal grief and no set timetable for passing through each of its phases. Because the emotional pattern of widowhood is such an individual experience, marked only by a personal sense of how *you feel,* the chronology of this book should not be used as an indicator of whether or not you're in the right stage at the right time. There isn't any right stage or right time.

But I can tell you, absolutely, that as a widow you will experience each of these stages. You cannot deny your anger or guilt or depression and jump ahead to recovery. Grief is a healing process that takes time. If you try to avoid your grief—turn yourself away from it or pretend it doesn't exist—it will only remain that much longer.

Unresolved grief is recognized as a forerunner of a wide range of physical, mental, and emotional disorders. The statistics vary, but most studies seem to agree that the widowed person is at greater health risk than the nonwidowed person. One study, by Kraus and Liliensfeld, that was reported in *Bereavement: Reactions, Consequences, and Care* (National Academy Press, 1984), tells us that the mortality rate for widowed persons under age forty-five is seven times higher than for nonwidowed persons. It is interesting to note that widowers have an even higher mortality rate than widows. Whatever the numbers are, resolving grief is not something to take lightly.

> We have known about my husband's illness for nearly two years, and we know that eventually he will die from it. I'm so filled with anticipatory grief and my fear has been going on so long that I often feel absolutely desperate. I'm in counseling, and it helps a lot, but I wouldn't wish this horror on anyone.

THE NEEDS OF THE GRIEVING

I want to focus here on some of the things to be learned from the changes that have occurred in grief counseling that can lead you on a more direct path toward acceptance and renewal. I discussed this subject with two staffers at Calvary Hospital in the Bronx, New York, Sister Catherine Seeley, coordinator for bereavement services, and Colleen Scanlon, psychiatric nurse clinician. They stressed, and I want to caution, that no one has discovered a miracle cure for grief. Some things have not changed very much. One of them is the overall impact of death. The word "impact" describes the effect so well. It means, literally, "to force tightly together"; "to be hit with a force"; and "the force of a collision." I'd say that's an accurate picture of what was happening to me underneath the brave act I put on. I collided with the truth. Martin was dead. I was alive and left to carry on my life. The facts of death haven't altered, but there is a new and deeper awareness of the way we can mend ourselves in the aftermath—and even before death occurs. It is now an accepted fact that the widow who is involved in her grief and who is guided through it will adapt better than the widow who does not acknowledge her grief. If you learn about bereavement, if you make the effort to understand yourself and your grief, you may be able to avoid some of the mistakes I made.

For years I've referred to myself as a negative role model. I think that the story I told in *Widow* and continue to tell here has helped a lot of people because it's a shining example of many of the things a person can do wrong. One reason is that I had no idea what was happening to me, and I had no one to tell me.

Perhaps in the future there will be some guidelines for people in our particular situation—that is, when a man dies immediately from an accident or heart attack. There must be great shock and grief, but it must be like pulling a tooth out real fast. Just better to get it over with and start recovery. When you must watch someone you love die by inches and deteriorate, the feeling of helplessness and guilt is overwhelming.

MY GRIEF IS WORSE THAN YOURS

Without a doubt, there is no event in our lives more unhappy to experience or difficult to accept than the death of someone we love. I know that firsthand. A death, a phone call, and my life was forever changed. I never expected that anyone could ever feel or understand the private hell of Lynn Caine—not my children, not my mother, and not my friends. No one had it worse than me. I was convinced of that. Most widows I have known have been convinced of it, too. Everyone thinks they have it worse than everyone else. I actually had a widow argue with me about it once. She said indignantly, "All the literature reports that sudden death is more terrible than having advance knowledge. It's harder on me because it happened without warning. At least you knew what was coming. You had fourteen months." Another widow wrote that she received condolences that said, "You're young. You'll get over it and marry again." She said, "How could anyone think such a thing? We had so little time together. It's not like we had years and years like most women do." Still another widow received a note that said, "How lucky you are that he went quickly. It must be a comfort to you that he didn't suffer." She told me, "If only I could have been with him when he died. It's worse when you don't know it's coming."

I'm not interested in promoting competition among widows. I think it's a waste of energy and not very helpful to anyone. But I do think it's important for all of us to understand that each death brings its own specific

10

problems and hardships. There is no "better" or "worse" way to lose a husband. Your age, your husband's age, the nature of his death, your economic status, your level of independence, whether or not you have children and how old they are, your own state of health, and many other variables *do* make a difference. There is value, I think, in recognizing what a woman faces when she must watch her husband die slowly over many months, as I did, and in understanding the intensified shock that comes from a sudden death, when a woman's husband leaves for work in the morning and never arrives there. What rule of measurement can judge which of these is worse? None. I want to emphasize again that this is not a comparison, but a discussion to inform you about the grief process and to give you insight into your own situation.

My husband was murdered by a complete stranger. I had come home from a Sunday visit with a friend to find that he had been shot and killed instantly. I had no chance for a last few words with him, no moment to express my remorse or regrets for some of the petty things I had said or done through our years of marriage.

SUDDEN DEATH

There is no prelude to sudden death. There are no good-byes, no last requests, no time to mend old fences or to say, "I love you." There is that thin moment that divides "here" and "not here," and there is notification that the person is dead. That's it. Perhaps because there's no time to grasp the reality before death, widows whose husbands died suddenly frequently need more time to grasp it afterward. Sister Seeley told me, "The initial shock usually lasts longer when death is sudden and there is a greater, more intensified period of disbelief. Most widows need to keep saying over and over again, 'This isn't real. It isn't real. I can't believe it.' The need to repeat it can go on for a long time, but the saying is the undoing of the illusion. Eventually, the widow is less and less convinced that it isn't real. There is also the intense aspect of resistance to confront the death at all and greater frustration and anger once the confrontation begins to take place. It's not uncommon for the full impact to settle in some eighteen to twenty-four months later. A widow often feels ridiculous because so much time has gone by, and she doesn't seem to feel any better. Everyone has been so helpful for the first year, and now she's into the second year. The personal support system isn't there for her, but the pain still is. Maybe suggesting that support is there for a year is an exaggeration. It's probably more like three or four months, or even less. I think that one of the greatest difficulties the widow of sudden death—and really all widows—faces is that we live in an impatient society, and too many people deal with the bereaved with a "time's-up" attitude.

I know of a widow whose husband died suddenly of a heart attack on their boat during a fishing trip. Her friends tried to clear out her sleeping quarters and dispose of sheets and towels and anything that might remind her of her husband. She became hysterical. Her friends meant well, I'm sure, but didn't understand that they were not helping her. Particular care must be taken not to rush yourself or allow others to pressure you into dismantling the things that represent a life together. This widow couldn't bear to part with the bed sheets. They still carried a body scent and were a link to her husband.

Another widow I met after a lecture in Chicago told me that her family was in a car accident on the way home from Thanksgiving dinner at her mother's house. She said, "When I came to days later, [my husband] Manuel was dead. My oldest son was in a coma a hundred miles away. My other child was torn and bruised and stitched and baffled [and was in a hospital room] up the hallway from me. I was numb for many months. I spent two months with a psychiatrist who knew nothing about grief, or so it seemed. Finally, my family doctor put me in touch with a bereavement specialist who understood what I was feeling and helped me through it."

One of the things I have learned from the many widows I've come to know over the years—and from those who work with them—is that the best medicine for the dramatic impact of sudden death is to get yourself into a bereavement group or personal counseling, and the sooner the better. I will say it here and many times throughout the rest of this book: There are plenty of resources and self-help groups and referral services available all around you. Even a lack of money is no longer a reason not to get help when you need it.

My husband was ill for nearly ten years. Most of our friends never knew it because he rarely talked about it. Maybe he was lucky that his cancer allowed him to appear normal, although I came to recognize that deathly gray pallor. But he played tennis and fished and to outsiders seemed fine. In some ways that made it tougher on us. I think we supported his looking fine by sometimes pretending that things were fine.

ANTICIPATORY GRIEF

When there is advance knowledge of a terminal illness, there is time for early counseling and planning and for setting things in order. At most hospitals and hospices today—and in acute-care specialty facilities like Calvary Hospital—the family is really an extension of the patient. In many places, there is an emphasis on allowing patients and their families to verbalize whatever needs they might have. There are family support groups and initial family conferences as well as patient discussion groups.

Anticipatory grief is sorrow and grief in the early stages of accepting the reality that someone is going to die, and it is ideally set in motion at diagnosis. There are people who

15

think it's morbid, but without hesitation I can tell you that if I could turn back the clock, I'd be the first one on line to take advantage of such counseling. To have spoken openly about my fears and sadness would have been a relief that I did not realize until long after Martin died. But as I've said, everyone deals with grief differently, and no one can say that anticipatory grief, even under the guidance of a professional staff, will lessen, or shorten, or eliminate the process of bereavement after death. A friend of mine who had time to prepare for her husband's death told me of her experience. Her husband died of heart disease. "One afternoon he just quietly went to sleep and never woke up," she said. "He had been in failing health for some time, but a month before he died he seemingly became better, and I was lulled into false hope, so the shock of finding him was twice as bad."

When you know someone is seriously ill, there are certain subtle—and other not so subtle—changes that go on during the time before death. There are doctor bills and personal details to be taken care of. They serve as a reminder that life isn't going to continue the way it used to. There are physical changes, which are reality indicators. But in

16

some cases, as with my friend's husband, the person doesn't look ill, even though he's dying. The absence of physical changes betrays what's really going on, and patients may not get the kind of response they expect from their family. People may treat them as though they're in good health because they look like they are, and they may be expected to conduct themselves as healthy people. In such cases, it can happen that no matter how much reality is fed in, the widow responds, "This cannot be true." The shock of death seems almost as great as if there had been no foreknowledge at all.

Another issue surrounding anticipatory grief is that with the knowledge of illness, people's relationships tend to intensify. Your husband may be dying, and now you will care that much more deeply and become that much more conscious of every need, which strengthens the marital bond. When he actually dies, the closeness that has resulted from knowing ahead of time can make the final separation of death more difficult. There is time to prepare, but there is also time to suffer.

They told me that he was brain-dead and that he was going to die. I sat in his hospital room and begged him not to die. I told him he couldn't do this to me and the children. I had three weeks to prepare myself, and believe me it might as well have been three seconds. I was not prepared at all.

I never actually said good-bye to Martin, but part of anticipatory grief *is* getting ready, saying good-bye, and with professional guidance, people are encouraged to do this. But it can happen that everyone is ready and has had the opportunity to say what they want to say, and then the death doesn't happen. Some of us are taught to believe in miracles, and who wants to take that away? Colleen Scanlon told me, "It's a tug-of-war sometimes. How do you remain in a relationship with a dying person and also prepare yourself for his death, which is going to mean some distancing." That's a tragedy that no one has the answer to. The waiting. When will it end. I felt it, but it was never explained to me. If it had been, I would have known why I was feeling the way I was, and that in itself would have been a comfort to me.

But for all that we can do, when death finally comes, many people respond by saying, "Well, what happened? What do you mean he died?" Intellectually, they have known all along that it would happen, but emotionally, there is still some time necessary for the reality to sink in.

I was in shock when my husband died. I mean, I was like one of those androids you see in science-fiction movies. They don't eat or cry or feel any human emotion at all. I managed to get by for almost two months like that. Then the pain hit me.

CLOSURE

The things that initially help the truth become real are the rituals that traditionally signal death. Condolence cards, memorial services, family gatherings, the headstone, the funeral—or whatever other ritual your religion or belief system includes—contribute as additional reality indicators. All the events that surround the formal time of mourning play an extremely important function by allowing people a time and place to share grief with others. The rituals give widows an environment in which it's socially acceptable to display grief. These things signal an end. They give us a strong message that a death really has taken place. I have heard it often from divorced women that until they had the document in their hand, the actual divorce papers, there was still an illusion that the relationship would be repaired. Although death and divorce are different, there is one similarity in that widows, too, need reinforcement. The headstone is one thing that fulfills such a need. It's like the period at the end of the sentence. It's a very dramatic moment because you see literally etched in stone that your husband has died. Each message of condolence I received said it over and over again. "We're sorry Martin died." "You have my sympathy for the loss of your husband." "I heard that Martin died, and I, too, will miss him very much." It's tough to go through all of these things, to read them, to hear them, to see them, and to respond to them. Their message is final, and that's exactly what makes them so valuable to you.

Over the last twenty years, I've learned a great deal about widows and their grief. I know more about despair and guilt and depression and anger than I ever wanted to. I know what you face and how difficult it can be at times. I also know you have courage and strength that you may not realize you possess. It probably doesn't seem possible that the day will ever come when you'll feel better, but it will.

Using this book, you'll learn many ways to help yourself. I can't promise that it will take away your pain, but I can say for sure and from experience that understanding grief will make it less confusing and less frightening. This book is meant as a practical and emotional resource for comfort and for help, no matter where you are on your way to recovery.

2

DISORIENTATION AND DENIAL

Dear Lynn,

I lost my husband seven months ago, and half the time I know that I appear sane to others, but I feel I'm going up and down like a yo-yo. Sometimes I think I'm going crazy. It comes and goes. I can remember the first time it hit. It was the day after my husband's funeral. I'm embarrassed to say that after everyone had gone home, I painted my kitchen cabinets because that was the weekend my husband and I had planned to do the job. A month later, without thinking, I sent two of my husband's suits out to be cleaned. Why? I wish I knew. It scares me when I suddenly realize that I'm acting as though my husband is still alive. I "know" he's dead. I just can't "believe" it. I have to concentrate hard to remind myself that he won't be home for dinner tonight, tomorrow, or ever and I don't have to buy food for two, but I keep slipping back into some weird daydream that any minute the phone will ring and he'll be calling to say he's going to be late. I wait for it to happen. I think I'll find out that this has been just a nightmare, that I'll wake up and my life will be real again. I guess that's it, things aren't real anymore. The only thing that would make it real again is having my husband back. I'm honestly worried that I'm losing my mind. How do I stop myself from doing things I know are crazy?

Widowhood shakes the foundation of your life, and it can take a long time for the reality of death to penetrate. It's no wonder widows feel disoriented, as though the rug has been pulled out from under their feet. It has.

I came to call the feelings of disorientation and denial and the accompanying confusion "the crazies," and with good reason. I lost things—everything I needed to function— such as eyeglasses, wallets, keys, money, checkbooks. I'd find myself dialing Martin's disconnected office phone number before I'd remember that he is dead. And I constantly followed men on the street who looked like him. I did things no one in her right mind would do. There were times when I thought I had taken leave of my senses altogether.

Though I didn't realize it then, my life was completely out of control. I had no idea how or where to start putting things back into some kind of order. I felt like the world had exploded, and my job was to find all the pieces and make them fit together again. I was overwhelmed by and unable to cope with the task.

There was no one to tell me to stay still, to make no major decisions, to maintain the status quo until I had regained the ability to think clearly again. Instead, I made the classic widow mistake. I uprooted myself and my children and made a disastrous move from the city to the suburbs. In my craziness, I thought that because my life had changed, *I* had to change my life as well. I thought that by making major decisions I could force my life back together again. I couldn't have been more wrong.

I didn't know then what I can offer you now: The wisest course of action is no action. For a time, anyway.

If only someone had told me to stop—to

wait—to let myself grieve. That's the best advice. I've only now, much belatedly, realized how much damage I've done.

Feelings of disorientation and denial are a predictable part of grief. They are a temporary—and I emphasize the word "temporary"—response to an intense emotional trauma. So it's a good idea to put off any big decisions—such as selling your house, moving, or changing jobs—until you adjust to the way your life has been altered. You lived with your husband, and now you're a widow. It takes time to integrate the major differences that death brings.

There are people who study the reactions of those who have had intense experiences— earthquake, rape, airplane crash, death of a loved one—and they conclude that it is normal for a person to be unable to gather his or her wits immediately afterward, that personal resources are shattered for a time, and that reality is distorted. The disorientation occurs for widows because what was once predictable and familiar in life becomes strange and unreal. The routine of living with another human being is upset. How is it possible that he's gone? Out of habit, we sometimes continue the old routine until we're able to reorganize our lives. It's like the amputee who has lost a leg or an arm and frequently can "feel" the missing limb, as though it's still there. Many years ago I met a young widow in southern California. She told me that her husband was a Vietnam veteran, a victim of a land-mine explosion that resulted in his losing an arm. She said that she had never fully understood the anguish he experienced when he would react as though his arm were still there. As a widow, she felt a similar kind of empty space and had difficulty adjusting. She said, "It took a long while for the internal me to catch up with the changes that had occurred outside in my life."

You can suddenly find yourself doing things almost automatically and feel confused and bewildered because the old life doesn't fit anymore. It can be a frightening moment when that realization hits you.

Denial is a way of screening out unpleasant thoughts and things that are disagreeable in your reality. It's a defense mechanism that helps a widow escape from an intolerable situation. It has gotten bad press though, and the truth is we need it for a while. Otherwise the changes can be too overwhelming. Denial actually makes you feel better, temporarily, because it protects you from facing the finality of the death of your husband. But when left unchecked, it can produce deep emotional conflicts because it's a very thin shield. *Denial is not truth,* and without truth the healing you need won't occur. If you allow yourself to stay in a dream world, it will take a lot longer to heal.

Inevitably, the avoidance is worse than the pain itself, more difficult, more destructive, more time- and energy-consuming. Avoidance just isn't worth the effort it takes.

I remember reading about how Queen Victoria acted after her beloved Prince Albert's death. For years, she slept with his nightshirt. Every evening, she would have his clothing laid out, and day after day, hot water was brought for his morning wash. It shocked me to know those things because, early on, strange as it may sound, I modeled myself after a stoic, brave Queen Victoria.

A widow from Texas wrote me, "Every night at six o'clock I hear my husband's key in the lock. Even though I know he's dead, I keep expecting him to walk through the door. Am I going crazy?"

I wish someone had told me to sit tight. I thought I was sane, but I was completely inconsistent and crazy! I went the route of setting the table for the wrong number of people, always including my husband, and of buying his favorite foods at the market. I'd forget to do things that were his responsibility and even forget to do the things that were mine. For a long time, I simply didn't know which end was up. It scared me.

Another widow, whose husband had been sick for three years before he died, said that she kept hearing him call her for help for months after he died. She thought she was going crazy, too.

I wasn't, they weren't, and you aren't. There's nothing shameful about the temporary insanity you feel from denial and from disorientation. I used to feel so foolish and stupid when I'd lose things or when I'd find myself standing in the living room calling Martin's old office. And I felt really dumb when I came to my senses in New Jersey, living in a place where I didn't want to live and not knowing how I could have made such a ridiculous mistake. I know now that it is part of the grieving process you go through as a widow. *Remember,* the feelings won't last forever. In the meantime, there are some positive steps you can take to get through the crazies without turning your life inside out and without making bad decisions that you must pay for later.

STARTING OVER

One of the keys to putting your life in order is to plan and create a structured environment for yourself. I read an article some time ago that discussed the aftermath of a tornado in Kansas. People who had lost their homes were interviewed, and when they were asked what comforted them most after the storm, many answered that it was the sound of an electric chain saw. I wondered about that for a moment—thought it was odd— and then bells of recognition went off in my head. For them that sound represented structure, rebuilding. It was the sound of life returning to normal. It certainly wasn't a cure for the loss of a home, but it helped the victims of the tornado start doing something about their situation. It motivated them to initiate cleanup operations, to gather community resources, to take inventory of what they had to work with, and to pull themselves together. So creating structure in your life is the first step to starting over.

KEEPING TRACK OF
WHAT'S IMPORTANT

Each morning, sit down and make a detailed list of everything you have to do that day. Include things that don't seem important enough to write down. Make shopping lists, a phone-call list, a bill-paying list, an errand list, and an appointment list. Also include a decision-making list. It will force you to review options and really think things through before acting. Add to that list the names of people who can help you make decisions: your lawyer, best friend, pastor, sister.

Then choose two or three things that are the most urgent for you to take care of. This determines your priorities and will help set up what you will do each day. When you have chosen two or three entries from your list, take at least one step toward taking care of each of your priorities.

The next morning, sit down and write the list again. Do it every day. When you accomplish something, mark it on your list or cross it out as each task is completed. This will give you the feeling that you are making progress, which you are, and will help you to be busy doing things that need to be done.

After a while, you'll probably find the daily list stretched to two days and then three. Finally, you'll be planning a week or so in advance as a natural outgrowth of planning one day.

It was eighteen months before I knew what hit me and faced the reality of life without my husband. Delayed grief reaction, they called it. I called it hell. When I was totally convinced that I was losing my mind—for what sane person does crazy things like kicks a beloved's grave, eats enough to gain forty pounds, walks all night in circles around a room, and holds the dog for hours. I stopped just short of self-destruction and tried a psychiatrist and joined a support group for widows, too. It took a long time for my pain to come out, but they listened and understood and kept saying, "You're OK, you're OK." I'm only starting to believe it now.

I've always stressed the importance of ac-

31

cepting help from others. Talking about your feelings of disorientation and stating those experiences of denial out loud can also bring structure back into your life. When someone says to you, "It's normal, you're OK," it really means something.

FINDING A CONFIDANT

You need someone to talk to, and the only way to do that is to reach out and ask for help. It's important that you share your feelings in order to understand them. Don't be afraid to show your vulnerability. Nonjudgmental, uncritical friends and relatives who are capable of responding will give you the love and understanding you need.

According to Colin Parkes and Robert Weiss, the authors of *Recovery from Bereavement* (Basic Books, 1983), the bereaved must confront "every element of the loss until the intensity of the distress is diminished to the point where it becomes tolerable, and the pleasure of recollection begins to outweigh the pain."

In order to accept loss and begin recovery you need sympathetic listeners. If you can't find them in your own circle, join a widows' group, or contact your local church for a lead. But find a way to talk it out.

> Not to be dramatic, but the majority of my life was spent with one person, who is now gone. I even find it hard to say he's dead.

When Martin died in 1971, widowhood was hidden in the closet. Death had replaced sex as the ultimate taboo, and no one talked about it. The only widows I knew were older women—my mother, my aunts, my friends' mothers. All of them observed strict death etiquette. They kept their feelings to themselves. Expressing grief was bad form. Consequently, I had no role model and was not easily able to talk about my fears of going crazy. Dignified silence was the order of the day, and I was determined to be the bravest widow since Queen Victoria. That was before I found out that she wasn't as brave as she acted either.

But I was bursting with unexpressed emotion, exhausted from putting on a brave front. I couldn't sleep. I couldn't concentrate. I became touchy, irritable. I suffered from anxiety attacks and was convinced I was going insane.

As my discomfort increased, I was forced to develop coping mechanisms. One of them was writing.

I did a lot of writing at all hours, which helped, but later when I reread it I couldn't remember even writing it. It was the craziest stuff.

KEEPING A JOURNAL

I kept a stack of yellow legal pads on my nightstand, and every night when I was unable to sleep, I'd confide in my "paper psychiatrist" all of the thoughts and feelings I tried to squash down, such as

how I hated Martin for dying, for abandoning me with two little children to raise alone and with no money;

how I resented the children and wished someone would take them off my hands;

how I missed love and sex and feared that part of my life was over;

how I resented married couples who excluded me now that I was alone;

how I couldn't cope with things and just wanted to die.

Here we are over fifteen years later, and a study has recently been done on the value of keeping a journal. The research project was conducted by Dr. James Pennekaer of Southern Methodist University in Dallas. For five days, fifteen adults were divided into two groups. Half were asked to write about disturbing life events and how they felt about them. The other half also kept journals, but wrote about more superficial topics and stayed away from any deep feelings. As a result, the group that let it all hang out on paper—describing disturbing events and the emotional feelings that went with them—showed strikingly improved immune function, based on blood tests. Those who stuck to the more trivial writing had no such improvement. I'm not surprised at the results, and I'm pleased someone took the idea seriously enough to study it.

If you have trouble expressing your feelings or there's no one available when you need to talk—or even if you do have a support group or a mental-health professional to work with—I recommend talking to yourself in the form of a journal. I know from the huge volume of mail I've received that writing can be therapeutic for every widow. I've lost count of the number of letters that include the line, "I don't know why, but I just feel better having written to you, getting some of this down on paper."

My paper psychiatrist helped me define my emotions and chart my progress. My journal became a close friend with whom I could share my deep hurts and fears. It helped me to sort out my thoughts and start thinking more clearly. I found great relief in recording my feelings every night.

Your journal doesn't have to be formal. You can write it as a letter to a friend if it's more comfortable. A yellow lined pad was my paper psychiatrist many times, and with that nightly visit I began to understand my behavior better and to release some of the pain I held inside.

One moment I felt I had everything I'd wanted all my life; in the next minute it was gone, shattered, never to be regained. I sometimes still deny my reality and fantasize the recreation of my marriage. I live in a dream world in which I keep telling myself, "If you can't face something, you look the other way." I feel like my life doesn't exist.

REALITY TOOLS

A widow whom I met at an airport told me that she would never forget the absolute confusion she felt the first time she had to take her car to the car wash. It wasn't that she had never done it before or that she didn't know how, but that it was usually her husband's job. She said it was difficult to put into words, but that it felt as though *she* had somehow changed. The world had remained the same and didn't acknowledge the change in her . . . "Weird," she said. She couldn't get the car in gear; she kept going in reverse instead of forward. One of the attendants yelled at her, but she just couldn't get herself together. She felt hazy, dizzy. . . . "Confused," she kept saying. "I was so confused. I forgot where I was. I imagined my husband was there and then remembered he was dead. I was terrified," she said.

I understand her confusion only too well. I felt it in my living room, on a city bus, in my office. I told her about some of the focusing exercises I had developed to snap myself back into reality. Over the years, I've improved on them and even taken some cues from sports psychology.

STOP-AND-FOCUS EXERCISES   The purpose of these reality tools, as I called them, was to bring myself back into the present, to become aware of my immediate environment, to feel the world as solid around me again. Counting was one way, slowly reciting . . . one . . . two . . . three . . . until you reach ten. Another tool was to describe for myself exactly what I was doing at that moment, to focus on the present. I'd say, "I am sitting on the sofa in my living room, and I am drinking a glass of water with ice." I'd do this for a few moments, describing my surroundings, sometimes even what I was wearing. Anything that would lock me into the present, that would anchor me, became part of the description.

Another exercise came from reading about the difficulties athletes have performing under intense pressure. Feeling tension and anticipation and trying to stay alert for long periods of time interfere with an athlete's ability to concentrate on the task at hand.

Paul Presthy, a veteran of Olympic pentathlons (an event that involves fencing, horseback riding, pistol shooting, a four-kilometer run, and a three-hundred-meter swim), which gives the athlete a lot to deal with, has found a way. In order to continually be able to focus attention when he needs to, between events he sits with a towel over his head and with his eyes closed, mentally building a dart board. He imagines that he is drawing a large circle and places the number 10 inside it. Then he draws another, smaller circle inside the first and moves the 10 into the new circle and places a 9 in the outer circle. Next, he draws another even smaller circle, moves the 10 in there, moves the 9 into the next-larger circle, and puts an 8 in the largest circle, and so on. It's a demanding sequence and requires complete concentration. But with practice, it can really improve your ability to work through feeling disoriented with less and less emotional trauma.

Still another way is to mentally say, "Stop." I started using this nonverbal jolt after I realized I had gone nearly two blocks out of my way, while following a man down the street who looked like Martin. I was surprised, but it worked.

One of the decisions that I made in my confusion was to return to school. I had had no college and had been out of school for twenty-three years. The tears used to roll down my cheeks as I drove to school; I could not concentrate. I was confused by the noise. I made dreadful grades. I stayed in school because I really wanted to, and eventually things got better. I began to make the dean's list. I had wonderful support from my family, friends, my teachers, and my therapist. Sometimes I still feel lonely and lost within, but I'm functioning much better than I was.

FINDING BALANCE

Many widows work hard to avoid pain, as I did. A friend of mine who is a bereavement counselor simplifies it by breaking down the avoiders into two groups: runners and sleepers. The runners deny death and the pain of loss by doing everything but being alone with their own thoughts. They look like they're conducting their lives well. They're accepting invitations, socializing, racing in four directions at once. Everyone admires the runner because she seems to be going on with her life.

The sleepers retreat and try to sleep through it all. They may take medication and just disconnect from everything for as long as they can. I'm not suggesting that you go against a doctor's care and not take medication that is prescribed, but you can't run or sleep forever. At some point you have to stop and feel.

Being able to find a balance between the two demands its own hard work and is part of the ongoing process that you're in. But I found another positive way to work through disorientation and denial that may help you. It's a way of using time that requires being awake and not running at high speed. It requires that you feel involvement and commitment and, most importantly, that you set a goal for yourself.

Every seminar I ever conducted had at its core the need for the participants to set goals. I believe in them, not as distracters, but as a way to stay in the moment, to focus on the present. If you feel committed to something and put your energy into it, you'll find that before long you'll be focusing on rebuilding rather than on loss. That is a major shift for a grieving woman to make. The goal you choose is entirely up to you. I always suggest that widows begin with an interest, something you'd *like* to do, something that attracts you. You can be just as committed to getting a job or working toward a promotion as you can be to doing volunteer work, planting a vegetable garden, or learning to speak a foreign language. You may have to push yourself a little to get started, like the widow who went back to school because she really wanted to, but it's worth it.

If you start with a piece of paper and write at the top, "Things I'd Like to Do," and make a little list, you'll begin to give yourself some direction and maybe even discover a goal that will surprise you. It doesn't have to be a goal that requires a huge accomplishment. Going back to school is a big commitment, but filling your time with even simple things that are important to you can be very uplifting.

A widow I know made a list like this and came up with an idea that had been forgotten long ago. She always wanted to learn how to drive a car, but lived in a city where it wasn't really necessary, so somehow she just never got around to it. She signed up for driving lessons, and after the second try at the driving test she got her license. I can't tell you how overjoyed she was. She told me that six months before this, she had been one of the sleepers. "I didn't want to do anything," she told me. "I wanted to be left alone in my bedroom hiding under a pillow. It was my daughter who tried to help me find my way out of my hiding place. She had been to a career counselor who suggested goal setting as a way to get where she wanted to go in the business world. She suggested that I do the same, but her idea was just to get me out of the bedroom. That's when I remembered the driving. Once I had the license, my next goal was to drive by myself to visit my daughter at college. It was over two hundred miles, and the other times I'd gone up to see her I had flown. I'll never forget taking my daughter and her boyfriend to lunch and driving them to a restaurant. What fun it was."

The point is that being involved in setting and achieving a goal is one of the ways you recommit yourself to life. It's a way to create a positive atmosphere in which you can begin to heal. It allows you to feel a certain amount of control over events again. And think about how much freedom the widow who learned to drive gave herself. I don't think I'll ever stop setting goals for myself. It's one of the best habits I've ever developed.

3

THE NEED
TO EXPRESS EMOTION

Dear Lynn,

My husband was killed in a car crash while we were on vacation in California eight months ago. We had just picked up a rental car and were on our way up the coast for some sight-seeing. It was the first vacation we had had together in a long time. I felt we were really just starting to live. We were both making money, had just bought a new home, and were planning to start a family. Out of nowhere, we were hit. I survived the crash with barely a scratch. My husband was killed instantly.

Everyone tells me that time will help, but right now it feels as though nothing will help. This hole in my life will never be full again. Why did he have to die when things were going so well? We could have been anywhere else that day instead of where we were. Why did he die and not me? Why was I able to get up and walk away from it and he wasn't? I feel like ripping up my entire house into little pieces and throwing it in the garbage because that's what's been done to my life. I don't remember ever hating anyone, but now I seem to be angry at the world. I walk around silent and everyone thinks I'm doing fine. I don't even cry and my friends think, "Isn't she strong." They don't realize how depressed I am. I wish I could cry. I wish I could scream my head off, but that's not the way I was raised. Sometimes I think I just can't contain it and that I'll explode. Sometimes I think I can't go on being strong for one more minute.

The expression of emotion is the most powerful way we have to communicate how we feel. Words carry emotion; a smile carries emotion; a quiet sigh carries emotion. We send out and receive emotional messages every moment of the day. But some emotions are easier for us to express than others. Laughter is an easy one. I've never heard of anyone ever seeking professional counseling because they couldn't laugh or because they were worried that if they started they'd never be able to stop. Social conditioning has a lot to do with which emotions we're comfortable expressing. My mother never said to me, "You better stop that laughing, young lady, or I'll really give you something to laugh about!" She did say it about my crying, though. We all find it completely natural to let go with a hearty chuckle from deep down inside when we see or hear something humorous. We don't even think about it. It just happens. It's an acceptable response. It feels good, too, and I'm sure that everyone would agree that it's healthy.

For widows who are struggling with their emotions, laughter is not the issue, although we could all use more of it during recovery from grief. The emotions that give us trouble are the very ones widowhood brings you face to face with. The feelings are unfamiliar, and there are too many of them. The intensity of it all can be overwhelming.

I've always imagined that the family grieves for several days after the funeral and then proceeds normally thereafter. Silly impression, but the deaths I've observed in my family have always been handled in that way. They're not big on

46

showing emotion, and I guess death is just something to be kept inside. That was before my husband died. Now keeping it inside has caused more pain for me than I ever thought possible.

When the numbness of early grief wears off and the fog begins to lift, many widows discover they're carrying around a warehouse full of sadness, guilt, depression, anger, and even hatred. You may ask questions like "Why me?" because you are the one who went on living, or "How could you leave me alone, expect me to carry on?" You may feel alternating and powerful urges of resentment and bitterness and the underlying feelings of hopelessness and helplessness that lead to depression. You may feel guilty and think, "If only I had said, or done, or held him, or been there with him." Widows experience feelings that many of us have had little practice dealing with. As one widow said, "I don't even know whom I'm mad at, but I feel like killing the world." It's difficult to know what to do with that kind of emotion. It's frightening to discover it in yourself. Sometimes we don't recognize where the feelings come from or why. Sometimes the feelings don't make any sense. How can you hate your husband for dying when you loved him for living? Unfortunately, for most of us, expressing these feelings isn't as easy as experiencing laughter, but we know that storing them inside isn't good for the body, the mind, or the soul. Many researchers suggest that unexpressed emotion can cause illnesses ranging from the common cold to heart disease and cancer.

I'm tempted to scream, but I'd probably blow the roof off. Mostly I keep from doing it because of what others might think. If I ever find myself in a spot where I'm sure no one would hear me, well . . .

STUMBLING BLOCKS

Many of us grew up fearing punishment for our emotional outbursts, and I guess it's the only way we learn any control at all. But maybe we go too far, especially with little girls. Women's liberation may have brought big changes in the lives of adults, but little girls are still not supposed to let go and scream or be angry. The result is that many women are extremely uncomfortable with anger, more so than with any other emotion. If we were all given permission to express emotions more when we were young or to be a part of the emotional times in the lives of our parents, we might not be so frightened of our feelings later in life—and we are frightened of them.

Some widows fear that if they start releasing the anger, the sadness, the boiling rage, the guilt, that they won't be able to stop. I've heard it many times: "If I start crying, I'll go on forever. The pain feels as though it will never go away." That's a fear that shields you from your own emotions and delays the healing process, and it simply isn't true. If you feel a need to cry, you should be able to. If you feel anger or other emotions that need a release, you have to find a way for that to happen. It won't go on forever. I can promise that. You'll stop when you're ready to.

Another stumbling block to the expression of emotion is that no one wants to be around you to witness it. It's a rare friend or relative who can take the emotional turmoil that is released through anger and sorrow. It's no reflection on the quality of a relationship, but the fact is most people don't want to experience the depth of your loss. Why would they? I didn't want to experience my own either. And so the feedback we get from early on in our lives—and for many of us, right up to the present—is that the expression of these powerful emotions is taboo. We learn to hold them back, to swallow them, to deny them, to express only what is acceptable, and to store the rest away.

In the normal, everyday events of our lives we find solutions. If you're upset or irritable or unhappy, you find acceptable channels for your feelings. You can talk things out if you're angry with someone. You take a deep breath and move on. We all have ways to cope that make us feel better. But when you're hit with the death of your husband, with the irretrievable loss of life, it's a different story. You can't talk face to face with your husband and tell him how bad you feel or ask him why the hell he left, and you can't cry on his shoulder.

If you feel burdened with the heaviness of emotion, it's time to give yourself permission to allow these feelings to emerge, be expressed, and pass. It sounds incredibly corny, but on the other side of the mountain that seems to sit in front of you, there really is a peaceful valley where you will find yourself again.

Anger as well as death is a no-no in our society. How many times have people looked at me and said, "Smile," when it was taking all the energy I had merely to keep going. How many times have people backed off at my expression of anger? Too many times, and it's taught me to hide it.

A PRICE TO PAY

"Martin, you bastard, look what I've been reduced to," I thought, as the cab went speeding down Fifth Avenue. I was returning home from a disastrous blind date, and I was angry. Oh, was I angry! It had started out fine, with a phone call from a man who sounded charming. I didn't feel ready to date, but a friend pushed and pushed, and then came the phone call. He sounded so nice I couldn't resist. I met him at a restaurant in the Algonquin Hotel, where I usually had business meetings. I felt safe there and was surrounded by people I knew in publishing.

He was fat and sloppy and had a pointy head. He told off-color jokes. "Why didn't I choose some dark, out-of-the-way place," I thought. "Everyone I know is here, and I'll

51

be seen." My heart sank. In those days, I compared all men to Martin, who was tall and thin and handsome. As I approached the table, I knew it was going to be a long night. "Lynn," I chided myself, "don't be so shallow. Give the guy a chance."

He really was a nice person, jokes aside, but he wasn't my type. I felt uncomfortable and wanted to go home, but to be polite, I stayed. He kept ordering drinks and just beamed at me and talked and talked and talked. I was belting down a lot of vodka and kept moving my chair farther and farther away from him. We had some dinner and more drinks, and finally I told him that I was tired and really had to go home. In the taxicab, he sat a little too close to me. I was terrified that he was going to make a pass at me and get physical, but he didn't. I don't think he had any idea of how I was reacting to him. He kept talking, but I was somewhere else. I was thinking about Martin and how if he hadn't died, I wouldn't be suffering this way; I wouldn't be subjected to this. He'd been dead only six months, and obviously I wasn't ready for this. I worked myself up into a real state of outrage and then ripped off my wedding ring, rolled down the taxicab window, and threw it out into the night. For the first time all evening, my date shut up. I'm certain he thought I was out of my mind, and I guess I was. I think he was very happy to drop me at home. Needless to say, I never saw him again.

The next morning, I realized what I had done. Filled with remorse, I walked back to where I threw the ring from the cab, about ten blocks from my house, and, of course, there was no sign of my ring. It was gone forever.

ANGER

It took me a long time to recover from that angry act, but I can look back at it now and understand that I didn't know what I was dealing with. I didn't know that the anger I expressed that night was a natural part of grief. The problem was that I was not in control of it. And anger isn't always expressed in such a dramatic way. It doesn't always come with a loud bang. Anger can be quiet, and any widow who has felt silent rage knows what I'm talking about.

Anger is protest. It is frustration at having lost something that cannot be retrieved. It can be the result of looking for a reason for death and not finding one. Anger can emerge because we need a place to put the blame for death—on doctors, family, friends, ourselves, God. I've heard many widows say, "I'm going to sue that lousy doctor for malpractice," when they know the accusation has no basis in fact. Widows experience anger because they are *widows*, and other women have husbands. We feel left alone, outsiders, and the world goes on as though nothing has happened.

Releasing anger or any other emotion that you feel is out of control is part of recovery, and that is the direction in which you want to go. When I thought about the loss of my ring, I felt terrible, but if anything positive came out of it, it was that I started to deal more constructively with my emotions—and not just anger. I vowed I'd never do anything like that again. It was too high a price to pay.

My lawyer says I've changed over the last two years. He says in "those" days he never could figure out what he had done to make me so angry with him. It's true, I treated him like the enemy. I never really understood why.

WORKING THROUGH IT

The way I expressed my anger that night was inappropriate, no question. It was not the right place or time or circumstance to vent my feelings. Had I been in touch with my emotions, understood them better, I would have known that I had to find another way to release them.

Some years ago I went to an Elisabeth Kübler-Ross workshop, and in one of the exercises, I stood in front of a bed that was filled with rolled-up newspapers. I was supposed to take a small rubber hose, which I still own and consider a trophy of sorts, and bash those newspapers. I beat the hell out of them, and it felt great. I could walk away feeling no regrets. It was harmless. I didn't hurt anyone. I was able to express my anger in a safe environment, and no one judged me for it. That is an example of using your energy—and anger is energy, pure adrenaline—with which to express your feelings. You don't have to bash newspapers, but you can use physical movement to release anger energy. It is appropriate to use it to wash a floor, punch your bed pillows, or exercise, perhaps by taking a walk or dancing. Movement helps to prevent the intense buildup of anger-energy that can peak in the form of some act you may regret later. Screaming at your lawyer is not an acceptable way, nor is throwing a temper tantrum in public. I don't think we change that much in our understanding of what is appropriate, and so you have to trust your own good judgment for knowing where and when.

It's best to use the anger at the time you're feeling it, but that's not always possible or appropriate. If not, you have to find a time and place. If you can't do it alone and you feel out of control, let others help you.

A widow from Oklahoma City wrote me that she would talk to her husband's picture when she felt angry. She'd set it in front of her and yell the most awful things. "Saying it out loud helped a great deal," she wrote. "I just poured it out and told him how rotten I felt and how mad at him I was. I'd usually end up in tears, but it got rid of the knot in my stomach. It really made me feel better." I've done this, too, and you might be surprised at how well it works.

I wish that I had been able to let the feelings show then. Now, with the aid of a psychiatrist, I am coming around. I think that maybe I will finally be able to work through the anger that I've bottled up for so long. We had so little time together. He was twenty-five for God's sake.

A WAKE-UP CALL

A widow I met in Albany, New York, told me a story of a different effect anger had:

"That whole summer following his death I kept stubbing my toes, or closing my fingers in the door, or burning myself at the oven. I dropped an iron on my foot and bruised it black-and-blue. Talk about clashing head on with reality. One night I had some friends over. I was feeling bad and was drinking too much. I wound up running right through the glass door that leads out to the patio. I was in the hospital for seven days. I started seeing someone to talk about my situation and finally realized that I was punishing myself for my husband's death. I was furious with him for dying and with myself for letting him. I was so angry that I literally started beating up on myself."

Anger is a very powerful emotion, and it can make you accident-prone. You tend to be so focused on your loss that you're not paying attention to what you're doing. This widow didn't listen to the message her accidents were giving her until she landed in the hospital. One reason is that she was drinking quite a bit. She told me that accidents happened when she was sober, too, but the drinking made everything much worse.

Alcohol mixed with anger or any other intense emotion can have a terrible effect. It can trigger rage, heighten it, and make you do things that you will be unhappy about later. The abuse of drugs falls into the same category. With all the conflicting emotions that you have to maneuver through, you don't need alcohol or drugs to make things more confusing. I'm sure that if I had had a clear head the night I tossed my ring, the evening would not have gone on long enough for that to happen. If I had been thinking straight, I would have simply excused myself early and gone home. The widow in Albany said she understood later that one of the reasons she was drinking was to numb her feelings, but her anger surfaced anyway. She said, "It crashed in on me. That glass door was a strong message for me to take a good, hard look at what I was doing to myself. I stopped drinking and got myself into therapy. I'm doing a lot better now. I haven't stubbed a toe or mashed a finger in months!"

I can remember that our family physician admonished me after six months. "Your period of grief is over," he said. "People will think you're crazy if you continue your depression." After that I felt something was really wrong with me. I found out later that he was wrong and that there aren't any set rules for getting through it. Everyone does it in their own time.

DEPRESSION

One of the most surprising responses I've received to my book *Widow* is from women who say they agree with everything in it *except* anger. They never experienced it, they tell me. My reply is to ask if they have felt depression. The answer is always yes. Some medical professionals say—and I agree with them—that unexpressed anger—or inner-directed anger, as it's called—turns into depression. It is hopelessness, resulting in such thoughts as, "What's the point? My life is over." It is helplessness, expressed through such feelings as, "I can't go on. I can't cope."

It can be the result of feeling guilt, of thinking, "I should have done more. I should have been able to save him."

Depression can surface as loss of interest in life, irritability, withdrawal, lack of energy, inability to eat or sleep or in some cases excessive sleeping, and at its most severe, inability to function. Depression can have a devastating effect on your health because it signals a kind of giving up. It is a temporary part of grief, to be sure, but it's important for you to be aware of what you can and should do about it.

It was without warning, and by the time I got from work to the hospital where they had taken him, he was dead. I never even got to see him and say, "I love you." This keeps haunting me, and I can't shake the recurring nightmare.

SEVERE DEPRESSION

One point that needs to be driven home is that depression can become a very serious problem for some widows. The more severe effects of depression can include a complete retreat from the outside world and sometimes thoughts of suicide. If you're feeling so depressed that you're not functioning, if the pain is too much, if the feelings are more than you can bear, you should seek help, if only from a friend. If you're in an emergency situation, there are suicide-hot-line numbers you can call. You're not alone. Help is available to you, and you *can* make it back. Don't give up on yourself.

Being able to say, "I am sad," and to cry seems to have great therapeutic qualities. I plan to give up my stiff upper lip—I, who was an example at family funerals.

GUILT

After a lecture I gave in Washington, D.C., I met a woman who had come back a long way from her depression. She had joined a widows' group and was doing fine, but that was a recent development. She had taken care of her husband during his illness, putting her life on hold for the year that she watched over him at home. She'd go out to the store and maybe to church once in a while, but that was it. When her husband died, she really couldn't believe it. She told me she had never fully accepted the fact that he was "terminal," and she thought that if she did everything right he'd pull through. After he died, she would run through the details of his death over and over again. She thought she might find some way she had slipped up, some small thing she could have done differently. "I started to feel like a failure, so guilty, and that my life wasn't worth living anymore," she said. "I was terribly depressed. I didn't answer mail or the phone. There were stacks of unpaid bills. It didn't happen overnight, but little by little, I retreated. I didn't know what to do about it. I kept thinking that I should have been able to save him."

Some widows repeatedly review each event leading up to the death. Whether it's a car accident, a fire, a terminal illness, a heart attack, whatever the cause, it's the same. Guilt, no matter what the reason, puts you in the position of somehow being to blame for what has happened. We set standards for ourselves, as this widow did, and when they can't be lived up to, we find fault with what we did or didn't do. You may think, "If only I hadn't insisted that he stop and buy the book I wanted, he wouldn't have been at the intersection when the truck went out of control. If only I had suggested the aquarium instead of the beach, he wouldn't have drowned." As one widow wrote:

I do believe the worst feeling of all is the quiet, when you think too much. If I had not done this or said that. If I had babied him more. If I had not allowed him to do things. If I had gotten a second opinion. If, if, if only.

Another widow told me that for nearly ten years she carried around feelings of guilt. "I was terrified when he had the first pains of heart attack," she said. "We were at the country house, and I couldn't persuade the doctor to come. When I came back from the phone, he had fallen to the floor. It was so awful, I couldn't budge him. I was petrified, didn't know what to do. I finally got through to emergency at about one-thirty in the morning, and eventually they arrived with oxygen machines. I should have known how to breathe down his throat. I was so afraid that I was helpless. The thought never left me that I should have done *something* to save him, but I never talked about it to anyone. Many years later, I met a doctor at a social gathering, and somehow it was possible to finally ask. I told him that I still walked around with the feeling that I should have saved my husband. He told me there was no way I could have helped. My husband died almost instantly of a massive occlusion. There was nothing anyone could have done. You can't imagine how relieved I was to get it out in the open and have the answer he gave me. If only I had known to speak up sooner. I didn't have to go around all that time feeling guilty."

I'll say again that this is a common reaction to grief. It's natural. Most widows experience it, and you're OK if you do. But it's healthy to talk about it as much as you need to, and you shouldn't put it off. Find friends, family, a support group, or a mental-health professional who is willing and able to listen. Communication is a positive way to deal with guilt feelings. But at some point you need to ask yourself, "Whose side am I on anyway?" You can't stay in an "if-only" state of mind and at the same time be focused on the future as well as on the healing that needs to take place. You have to make a choice. A spoken word, a past argument, and the events that led to death cannot be changed now. Give yourself a break, and recognize that the past is just that.

I was courageous, determined, and responsible, but I hated him. When he died I felt a weight lift off my shoulders. He was a rat and I'm better off without him.

WITHOUT GUILT

I shouldn't have been so surprised the first time it happened, but I was. A woman in one of my widows' groups sat up straight in her chair and quietly but firmly said, "I can't identify with the rest of you, because frankly I had a lousy marriage, and I'm glad he's gone." The other women in the group responded with horror. She certainly wasn't the usual picture we have of the grieving widow.

This woman dropped a bombshell right in the lap of the group. Another woman asked her how she could possibly feel that way. "I was married to him for nine years," she said. "He ran around on me. The icing on the cake was the affair he had with my friend and neighbor. After a while he returned home to me, as usual. A few months later he was diagnosed with inoperable cancer, and I took care of him until he died. I realize now that I must have been crazy to live with a man who ignored me or threatened to kill me if he had a bad day at the office. That is, of course, when he *had* a job. I never had a day of peace with that man, and I'm glad he's dead. I should have left him years ago."

The fact is there *are* widows who had rotten marriages, who suffered abuse at the hands of their husbands, and over the years I've come in contact with many of them. These widows often feel released from bondage rather than guilt or intense sadness. Even in good marriages, some women suffer from unresolved conflicts. The woman in my group was still sorting through her feelings, and her honesty was a big step toward healing. That's what a widows' support group is for. There are hot lines for abused women, and calling one of them would probably give you a lead for finding an environment in which you can explore your feelings. If you're in such a situation and need to talk about it, do so. You aren't alone.

At times I feel so depressed that I wonder if I'll ever be able to cope with anything again.

DOING FOR YOURSELF

When you direct anger outward you're saying, "What did I do to deserve this?" You're protesting. When you direct anger inward, you're usually not asking anymore, you're giving in. That's what being powerless and hopeless is all about—letting go, surrendering. "My life is over" is a perfect example of this kind of thinking. Many widows experience a period of depression, and so you should know that it isn't only you who feels this way. But you very definitely need to work on depression because it can be dangerous. Depression immobilizes you. You may feel that you just can't get up and do anything: write the check for the phone bill, tend to your children, get out of bed in the morning. You feel you can't do it, so it doesn't get done, and you may, little by little, back away from life. One widow described her depression to me as a shrinking feeling. "I seemed to get smaller and smaller," she said. "The outside world, the things that I should have been doing, got larger and more overwhelming. For a while, it all seemed insurmountable."

There are ways to work on your depression, but it's important to caution that these suggestions are not a cure. They will be helpful, but if you feel the depression is overwhelming you, it's wise that you find professional counseling.

- The first step is to acknowledge that you are depressed and make a firm decision to do something about it. *Action* is the word to keep in mind. If you're sitting under a blanket waiting for things to change, you'll be waiting for a long time. If you're suffering from depression, make the decision now that you want to *do* something about the way you feel.

- Don't defeat yourself by planning to change everything overnight. Working through your depression won't feel insurmountable if you start with small steps. Begin by allotting an hour or so each day to doing those things you've been putting off or have been unable to face. If an hour a day is too much, start with an hour every other day, but mark your calendar as though you have an appointment to keep, and stick to it. Be definite about the hour, and stop and do something else when the sixty minutes are up. If paying bills has reached a critical point, start by organizing the ones requiring immediate payment, and write out at least one check. If it's phone calls or correspondence that need attention, do the same. Obviously, if you're working, you'll have to schedule this time in the evening or on the weekend, as I did.

- At the same time you're allotting yourself an hour for things that need taking care of, also schedule one hour to do something you enjoy. Frequently, it's easy to be active if you're indulging in a pleasant activity. Start with a pleasure hour rather than a work hour if you want. Use that hour however you like, but plan ahead to fill it. Perhaps listening to music, spending an hour in a museum or library, or gardening is what you enjoy.

  Again, make it an appointment that you must keep. As often as you can, include a friend in your plans. To get started, it's better to leave the house rather than entertain in your home. An outside environment can make a big difference because you won't be as prone to refocusing on the depression.

- It's OK to spend some time alone, to retreat when necessary, and you can plan this time as well. Remember that "alone time" is something you've needed at other periods in your life, too. But if your isolation time is greater than your active time, then you have to work to tip the scale the other way. Pay attention to how much time you spend alone.

- Many widows tell me that physical exercise, particularly bicycle riding or jogging or even a brisk walk once a day, is a terrific boost to the lack of energy that can be part of depression. Your family physician should be in on the planning of any exercise regimen.

- Reaching out to others is another way some widows work through their depression. The world is full of volunteer programs, and you won't have to look far to find one.

- The need to work on yourself never

ends. If you try some of these methods and then find yourself slipping back, start again. It's important to be aware of how you feel and to act in a way that leads you back into the world, not out of it. You have to keep at it.

Finally, I stopped getting out of bed at all. I thought about suicide a lot, but I didn't have to. I was already killing myself. I thought my life was over. I'm so glad to be able to say now that I was wrong. I'm alive. I survived, and I'm proud of it.

SADNESS AND CRYING

A display of tears, more than any other expression of emotion, can make us feel vulnerable and defenseless. Tears reveal our pain and our sadness and touch the core of our being. They can also signal joy. Many tears have been shed at weddings and at the birth of children. Unlikely events bring tears, like the beauty of a sunset or the soft sound of music that fills you to the brim with emotion.

Tears are so wondrous and so full of mystery that there has been an ongoing study of them at the St. Paul-Ramsey Medical Center in St. Paul, Minnesota, headed by Dr. William H. Frey II. The project suggests that crying, like perspiring or any other excretory process, cleanses the body of toxic substances. One of the theories is that emotion stored inside the body can produce chemical changes, or an imbalance, resulting in people being sad, depressed, or angry, and crying is a natural way to correct the chemical balance. The study has also revealed that emotional tears are quite different from tears caused by an irritant, such as onions. Emotional tears contain more protein and many other chemicals, which appears to support the idea that the body really is getting rid of more substances when emotion is involved.

One of the problems with studying crying and tears is that it isn't all that easy to have people cry on cue or even to collect the tears once they're produced. The thing that has greatly interested me in this kind of research is how they get people to cry. I found that one of their methods exactly parallels what I've recommended to widows for a long time.

Crying comes more easily for some widows than others. It brings relief, but it can also make you feel humiliated, even frightened, at the loss of control. But the fact is, and I don't need any research project to tell me this: Tears can release the choked-up, filled-up, knotted-up feeling that widows experience as part of grief. You may have trouble bringing on the tears because of inner defenses, social conditioning, or fear, but crying can have a tremendous healing effect. If they come easily, fine. If you have to work at it, you should.

I wish I had wept, but I smiled and was strong, or so I thought. Now I believe it takes much greater strength to let it out.

HAVING A GOOD CRY

Many widows have told me that they set aside a special private time to cry. It's fine to spend time alone with your sadness and to plan ahead for it. You don't want to break into tears in the office or in the middle of a dinner party, and chances are you won't, if the need to relieve sorrow can be planned for privately. Here are some suggestions for stimulating tears:

- Some widows take out the photo album

and review past vacations and family gatherings. Others don't need that kind of stimulus, but can fill a bathtub and sit with their thoughts for an hour and sob. Still others tell me that they take a drive alone and park in some quiet place and just let it flow.

- A sad book can do it. I've reread *Wuthering Heights* more than once, and I think *Gone With the Wind* is a good one for stirring emotion, too.

- The best way I have found to open the floodgates—and this is the one the researchers use—is to watch a sad film. I did my own little survey among widows and came up with some real tearjerkers:

Terms of Endearment	*Camille*
Sophie's Choice	*Anna Karenina*
The Yearling	*The Great Santini*
The Elephant Man	*Brian's Song*
Born Free	*The Champ*
Harry and Tonto	*Dark Victory*
The Diary of	*Little Women*
Anne Frank	*City Lights*

You probably have personal favorites that you'll want to add to the list. The idea is that you can pick a time and place to have a good cry and be alone if you want to. If having a friend present is comforting and helpful, by all means do it that way.

I have never known of a widow who said she didn't feel better after crying. It isn't a cure for grief by any means, but it can relieve so much of what you hold inside. It's good to let go of it and move on to the laughter part of life again.

SUMMING UP

Emotions are so personal, so individual, that the best advice I can give is that you need to find a way to deal with them that works best for you. If you're suffering, it's most important to put yourself in a setting where you can express yourself without judgment or harm to anyone, including yourself. You need to allow yourself a time to be vulnerable. It can be with a friend or a relative, if that makes you feel comfortable. If there isn't anyone to turn to, you may need to look for a widows' group or a medical professional. The best way to find one is probably through your church or family doctor or through another widow. Pick your time and place to talk it out, cry it out, and yell it out, but you have to *let* it happen. A note I recently received from a widow states it well:

I found that time and the opportunity for expression helped enormously. I am grateful to let go of the bitterness. I haven't forgotten and I still grieve, but I'm feeling a hell of a lot better now. Living isn't nearly as bad as I thought it would be. Sometimes I actually find myself smiling.

4

SLEEPING AND EATING DISORDERS

Dear Lynn,

It's five A.M. and I'm wide awake. I never feel more alone than I do at night, My problem is sleep. I wake up more tired than when I lie down. Most nights I sit up in bed, eyes open, unable to sleep. I usually watch television and wait for the station to sign off for the night. They play the national anthem and show a flag waving in the breeze, and then a test pattern comes on for a while, and then nothing but static. That's when it's rough. I'm always tired anyway, even after I sleep the few hours I'm able to.

Just after my husband died, I remember sleeping all the time. I couldn't get enough sleep. My doctor told me that was normal, but now everything is different. Is this normal, too? Nothing feels normal. I'm jittery and tired and wide awake at the same time. I get stomach pains. I cry, and the tears feel like acid. I have no energy and I can't eat. The thought of food makes me ill. Sometimes I wonder if I might be dying, too, a little at a time. I know my children are having a hard time, too, but I can't seem to help them.

I can't remember the things I'm supposed to take care of at work. I can't remember what I'm supposed to buy at the store, and then night comes and I remember everything. I remember too many things. I pray for a night of peaceful sleep, but it doesn't come. I pray I can make a dinner and sit down and eat it, but I can't. I'm suffering. I feel rotten.

We spend most of our lives taking for granted our abilities to eat and sleep properly, and on a regular schedule. And why not? They're natural functions regulated by a reliable inner-body clock. When you're hungry, you eat. When you're tired, you sleep. Simple. But your body clock is sensitive, and a change in your life can throw it out of whack. Even something as simple as a change in season can affect it. If you've ever experienced jet lag after an airplane flight, you can understand how delicate the biological clock really is. Your watch may tell you it's dinner-time, but your stomach says it isn't. It may be dark outside and time for bed, but for you it's morning and time to be on the move. Eventually, you adjust to a new time and place, and the delicate balance of your body clock is reestablished. But if jet lag or a change of season can upset the balance, then widowhood turns it inside out.

For widows, the return to normal can be a much slower and more difficult process. Eating and sleeping are no longer taken for granted. Instead, they are things you wish for and pray for. We know that lack of sleep and food for any length of time is not healthy. So it is in your best interest to make an effort to improve the situation. Fortunately, there is much you can do.

I feel as if I died also, except I'm expected to eat and sleep.

GETTING A GOOD NIGHT'S SLEEP

My greatest dread used to be facing the night. I've lost count of the number of times I finally drifted into sleep just as my morning alarm was about to go off. I was in a vicious cycle of wanting to sleep when I needed to be awake and being awake when I wanted to sleep.

Every widow complains of sleep disturbances of one kind or another. Some women fall asleep the minute they get into bed, only to awaken with a start, trembling from a barely remembered nightmare. Some women can't get to sleep at all, and others sleep too much, which results in them having a groggy or listless feeling.

The disturbance patterns vary, but all amount to the same thing. The frustration of not being able to sleep the way you're used to creates tension and exhaustion.

What is considered to be a good night's sleep is different for everyone. For some women five hours is perfectly normal, but now that they're widows, they sleep ten or more and can't wake up in the morning. For other women, eight hours is the usual amount, but since their husbands' deaths, they can't seem to sleep more than two hours at a time. For most people, the average is seven to eight hours. If night after night you're not getting the kind of restful sleep you need, it's time to take some action.

I fall asleep early and then wake up and can't go back to sleep. I rest two hours and then I'm up. I'm always tired, but it doesn't seem to matter. I still can't sleep.

WHERE YOU SLEEP

Your bed is not the place to go over bills and legal papers or even to make a shopping list. If your bedroom doubles as a work space, change that arrangement right away. Having a desk in the bedroom will only remind you of unfinished work, unpaid bills, and unanswered mail. Use your bedroom only for sleeping. Move any paper work to the kitchen, den, or dining room. Remove anything else from your bedroom that might disturb you, even photographs, if necessary. Your bedroom should be a peaceful and relaxing place, so try to make your surroundings as pleasant as possible.

I've rarely met a woman whose sleep patterns didn't change after her husband's death, especially if she used to sleep with her husband in a double bed. My bed seemed to grow wider and longer without Martin, and that vast space made me feel very small and vulnerable. My heating pad was a comforting source of warmth when I started to sleep

81

alone. I didn't feel quite so uncomfortable in that large bed if I lay on my side with lots of pillows under my head and the heating pad on my stomach. They made the bed feel less empty.

I used pillows, but a widow from Alabama wrote, "Thank God for my cat. The softness and purring lulled me back to sleep on many a restless night." Studies have proved this to be true. It has been shown that the presence of an animal lowers blood pressure and generally produces a calming influence. She went on to say, "Having my cats nearby has helped me to feel I'm not the last living thing on the planet."

I met a widow at a lecture I gave in New Orleans who told me that there were times when she just couldn't face her bed at all. She'd sleep on the living room couch and even tried the floor a few times. I've done this, too. There's no point in forcing yourself to stay in bed when you can't sleep. If you don't fall asleep within ten or fifteen minutes, don't frustrate yourself by lying there staring at the ceiling trying to will yourself to sleep. Get out of bed and try sleeping somewhere else. There will come a time when the floor or couch will be uncomfortable and you'll want to get back to your bed.

I crash out early and then wake up again and can't go back to sleep. I never sleep more than two hours at a time. Sometimes I listen to the radio at night so I don't feel so alone.

PLANNING FOR WAKEFULNESS

You can be prepared for the times you wake up in the middle of the night and not be so overwhelmed with frustration at not being able to fall back to sleep right away.

Keep a pad and pencil by your bed. Simply writing down your thoughts can help to relax you. Never mind if they make sense or not or if they follow any logical order. If you find you're going through the same things again and again, as though there's a tape in your head running on a loop, write that down, too. It will help you to begin letting go of recurrent thoughts.

If thoughts are keeping you awake but you're not really alert enough to sit up and start writing, try giving yourself a mental suggestion that you will change your thoughts. Tell yourself that you are rewriting the script, that you're going to change the channel. Pretend your pillow is the channel changer and turn it over. It sounds absurdly simple, but it is effective.

Have some magazines nearby or a book, but choose light reading. I still do a lot of my reading before bed, and if I wake up during the night, I always have a book handy. More than one widow has written to me to say that she keeps a Bible on her night table for nighttime reading. Other solutions are to turn on the television or quiet music for a little while. Many widows tell me that a television left on through the night takes the edge off loneliness.

I hate the night. I can't sleep. Often I just wander around the house like a sleep-walker, but unfortunately I'm not asleep. I walk about wide awake.

PREPARING FOR SLEEP

What you do before you go to bed for the night can make a big difference in how well you sleep and for how long.

A warm bath or shower before bed will give you a head start. The warm water actually causes the blood system to flow to the outer parts of your body, which is exactly what happens when you start to fall asleep.

84

Try to slow down activity at least an hour before bedtime, and especially avoid things that require intense concentration. Give yourself a chance to unwind.

A small amount of mild exercise like yoga or an early-evening walk can help to relax you. But don't get involved in workout sessions before you go to bed. An exercise regimen is valuable at any other time of the day. It will help you to be physically tired when you're supposed to be, but won't help just before bed.

It's important to establish a consistent sleep pattern to encourage your body and mind to adapt to a regular sleep cycle. Try to go to bed at the same time each evening. It is equally important to set your alarm clock to wake you at the same time each morning.

Don't let yourself nap during the day. Instead, keep busy with something that requires your attention. If you don't have a job, plan an activity, something that will keep you occupied during waking hours.

L-tryptophan, an amino acid, is often called nature's sleeping pill. It's a nonaddictive remedy and has proved to be extremely effective in promoting healthy, restful sleep. It's available in tablet form in many health-food stores. Some doctors are critical of its use, however, so you might want to check with your family physician before buying it. A small amount of L-tryptophan is contained in milk, so the old remedy of a glass of warm milk before bed actually does work.

I always like a cup of herbal tea laced with lots of honey before bed. Celestial Seasonings makes one called Sleepytime, and Lipton's Special Moments is also quite good. Herbal teas, such as chamomile, work well because they don't contain caffeine.

My doctor kept me supplied with sleeping pills and tranquilizers. I honestly can take them or leave them. Now, at trying times I only take one tranquilizer at night sometimes to help me sleep. I only get five or six hours a night.

If you take sleeping pills, do so only under the advice and care of your doctor. Alcohol is not a recommended sleeping aid. Having a drink or two before bed to help you fall asleep is a bad habit to get into. Before you know it, one or two drinks aren't enough. If you're going to have a drink or a glass of wine, have it early in the evening. As habits, both taking pills and drinking alcohol can get out of hand, so it's wise to be cautious with your intake.

LIGHTS OUT

Once you've gone through whatever going-to-bed ritual you've set for yourself, you'll be receptive to the following sleep and relaxation exercises. I've used both of them and can tell you that they work.

Read them through a few times before you begin in order to familiarize yourself with each step.

SLEEP EXERCISE Close your eyes and make yourself comfortable. Begin by taking slow, deep breaths through your nose.

Breathe in . . . breathe out.

Breathe in . . . breathe out.

Continue breathing slowly—in and out—for at least a minute or two. Focus all your attention on each breath as you take it.

Feel yourself becoming more and more relaxed and sleepy with each breath. It's a pleasant sensation. Allow yourself to enjoy it.

Beginning at the top of your head and gradually continuing down to your toes, focus your attention on each part of your body.

Allow your breathing to relax each part as you go.

Start with your head—your forehead, your cheeks, your entire face—and let each part go to sleep, relax. Move to your neck . . . and then your shoulders . . . your back . . . your abdomen . . . your pelvis . . . your legs . . . and, finally, to your feet and toes.

When you're totally relaxed, just go with the feeling. As your deep breathing continues, you will become more and more sleepy. You will feel yourself drifting off to sleep, more and more relaxed and drowsy. Don't be surprised if you fall asleep before you reach the end of the exercise. It works like a dream.

VISUALIZATION FOR SLEEP A young widow I know combines visualization with the previously described sleep exercise. This one begins with your feet.

Close your eyes and slowly inhale through your nose; exhale through your mouth. Just relax and breathe slowly and easily.

With your eyes still closed, pretend you have an empty television screen in front of you. Visualize the borders of the screen and keep it blank.

When you have visualized the empty

screen, put a picture of your feet there, just as though you are seeing them with your eyes. Give yourself a moment to get a good, strong picture, and then imagine that there is lots of activity going on inside your feet.

Pretend you can see wheels turning and workers pulling levers and mechanical things moving all over the place, just like in a factory or a hustle-bustle business.

Once you have a picture of movement, begin to slow down the activity. Visualize the wheels and levers stopping their motion and the workers leaving the area. Everything becomes quiet and still, as though it's the end of a work day.

Keep that picture on your screen for a moment.

As the activity comes to a halt, you will feel tension leaving your feet. There might even be a tingling sensation.

Move up to your legs and repeat the exercise using your screen. Continue visualizing parts of your body on the screen, progressing from the pelvis to the back, arms, shoulders, neck, and finally the head, each time repeating the exercise.

This is an exercise that gets better each time you do it. Eventually, you probably won't even need the screen to do it, and visualizing gives you the extra advantage of clearing away the thoughts that may be keeping you awake.

I have a terrible time getting myself up in the morning. It's a battle. By the time I get to the office at nine, I feel exhausted. I've even spent lunch hours sleeping on the couch in the ladies' room. I feel groggy all the time, like I'm living under water.

WHEN YOU SLEEP TOO MUCH

For widows who have trouble falling asleep, it's hard to believe that the other side of the coin could ever be a problem. But it is. And it can be just as big a source of worry—I know. I can remember cowering under my blankets on many nights, wishing that it would stay dark forever and that I would never have to face the day. I even would pray that the sun wouldn't rise and the day would never begin. I was depressed and fearful, and I wanted to completely avoid anything and everything.

For many widows, the only safe place is the bed, so they retreat into sleep in order to stay there. There is a disorder called *ago-*

raphobia, a word derived from Greek that means, literally, "fear of the marketplace." The disorder doesn't necessarily apply to sleep problems, but the definition of the word certainly does. Sleeping too much is a way of blotting out the reality of grief, widowhood, the future, responsibilities, and a host of other things a vulnerable person often doesn't feel able to cope with. It is a natural reaction to depression and too much stress. Sleeping is easier than hiding in the closet, but maybe not so different. Certainly, there are healthful reasons for sleeping more than usual, but if you're sleeping the nights and days away and the weeks are passing by, it's a good idea to find a way to get yourself up and out of bed.

I don't know what to do about sleeping so much. I go to bed early and still can't get up in the morning. I get my children dressed and off to school and then go back to bed. Some days I never get up. My children have found me in bed at four in the afternoon. They're frightened that I sleep so much. They think something is wrong with me. I think something is wrong with me.

WAKE-UP RITUALS

Make sure you set your alarm for the same time each morning. A regular schedule helps your body to readjust. When your alarm goes off, get up no matter how tired you feel.

If your health is good and you've checked with your doctor first, a morning exercise routine is an excellent way to start the day. Even if you have to drag yourself out of bed, do so. Stand up and breathe deeply. Oxygen is an energizer, and deep breathing will get your brain to send a wake-up call to the rest of your body. Do five minutes of light stretching by reaching up as though you're climbing a rope that's suspended above you. Then stretch your arms out in front of you. Then extend your arms out from your sides and stretch horizontally left and then right. Jump up and down with your arms down at your sides. Just try to keep moving for five minutes.

If you have a backyard or a porch, walk outside. There's nothing like fresh air as a wake-up tonic. Even if it's cold and you have to put on a coat, give it a try. And if you have the time, take a short morning walk. Down the block and back is fine.

The visualization exercise given on page 88 can help you wake up, too, when done in reverse. Instead of imagining that all that activity is stopping, pretend that everything is revving up for the day. The following is another good visualization exercise to get yourself energized.

VISUALIZATION WAKE-UP When your alarm goes off, open your eyes and breathe in deeply. Exhale. Do this three times. Now close your eyes and breathe normally. Visualize a bright, beautiful yellow sun sitting just above your head. Get a good strong picture of it and imagine sunbeams shooting out from all sides. Now imagine that the sunbeams are shining down on you and enveloping you with wonderful, strong energy. Breathe some of it in. Let it move all around you, and feel just as though the warm sun is shining on your face. When you've given yourself a good dose of sun energy, pretend that the sun moves back into the sky where it belongs. You can pull it back each morning as needed, even on a cloudy day!

My whole body seems to jump in the way

to complicate what my mind is working on. I'm trying hard to get through this, to survive as a strong individual, but it's weird sometimes that I actually cannot eat. I can't force myself to. There's no point. My stomach jumps and tightens and feels like two pieces of sandpaper being rubbed together.

COMFORT FOODS

During my first months as a widow, my insides felt raw, sore, and bruised. I couldn't tolerate any roughly textured or highly seasoned foods or anything that requires much chewing. I didn't feel much like cooking either, but I certainly needed to eat. I wanted food that demanded no effort from me, food that would slip down my throat easily. I craved the softness of ice cream and the blandness of yogurt. I wanted the kind of foods my mother fed me during childhood illnesses. My energy level was very low for a long time, and I'm sure part of the reason was that I ate too many foods that did comfort me emotionally, but didn't give me the nutrition I needed. A widow from Salt Lake City wrote me that for months after her husband's death, the only food she could face was ice cream. "I became an ice-cream junkie," she wrote. "I was shocked at myself and gained a lot of weight, which only made me feel worse."

Early bereavement is a time to be kind to yourself and to your body, especially when it comes to food. But getting your life back in order and working your way through grief requires a great deal of energy, and you won't have it to give unless you eat properly. I eventually found that eating a combination of what I call comfort foods and smart foods is the easiest way to get the most benefits.

One day about four months into hell I awoke (very suddenly). The pain was incredible. I wouldn't wish it on my worst enemy. Raw is the word. My body ached with pain as though someone jammed me with a knife. I try to force a little food down every day, but it isn't easy.

Anything edible that will create a soothing effect comes under the heading of comfort foods. I've put together a long list of them during the time I've been a widow:

Applesauce with cinnamon or anything

with cinnamon—it was my magic
ingredient

Bananas

Warm bread; homemade or from the bak-
ery is best, but any bread lightly
warmed will do the trick

Creamy cheeses

Chicken soup or any other kind of soup,
especially "cream-of" soups

Hot cocoa

Custard

Scrambled eggs

Ice cream, of course

Warm milk with honey; also try adding a
couple of drops of vanilla or sprinkling
a little cinnamon on top

Milk shakes of all kinds

Oatmeal with brown sugar

Pastas with butter

Peanut butter right from the jar

Mashed potatoes; even the instant kind from a box is fine

Rice pudding or any kind of pudding

Yogurt with fruit or plain

Comfort foods require little or no effort but many of them shouldn't be used alone as a steady diet. Obviously, you can't live on ice cream, rice pudding, or milk shakes for long. But there were days when I, too, could face nothing else.

I didn't know much about vitamin supplements then or about liquid nutrients like Ensure Plus, which is a liquid balanced meal and is available in health-food stores. If you're indulging yourself with comfort foods, choose the rest of what you eat with care. Even if you don't eat much, eat smart. Add something nutritious to every meal or snack you eat. If you're eating ice cream, add a little fresh fruit. Or if you're eating yogurt add a little chopped onion and chives and whatever

97

herbs you like, and dip fresh vegetables into it. I developed my own health drink by mixing in a blender one raw egg (egg yolks shouldn't be eaten more than three times a week, so this is not an everyday drink), a packet of Carnation Instant Breakfast and some milk (preferably skim or low fat). Soups are on the comfort food list, and they should be made nutritiously with lots of vegetables, or if that's even too much, throw the ingredients in the blender and make it a smooth, creamy soup.

Pay attention to what you eat, and try to prepare your meals yourself. It's unlikely that you'll want to get involved with lengthy recipes, but you don't have to. A can of chicken broth mixed with lightly steamed vegetables is nutritious and easy to make. Cooking for yourself is way of doing something special for yourself. It focuses positive energy on you, and it helps you improve your state of health. Additionally, prepackaged foods don't always have the vitamins you need.

You can encourage yourself to eat by planning a meal (even if it's ice cream for dinner) for regular times each morning, afternoon, or evening. If you avoid snacks—just as you avoid naps to minimize sleeping problems—

you'll have a better chance of being hungry on a regular schedule.

If you spend a few quiet moments relaxing before sitting down to a meal, you might find you can eat more. There's no point in forcing yourself to eat when you're feeling stressed. Concentrate on calming yourself before each meal. And try to make your dining area as pleasant as possible. It doesn't seem important, but setting a clean table and decorating it with a fresh flower or just opening a window and letting in some sunshine and morning air make food a lot more appetizing.

You'll slowly return to normal eating habits, but only you can be the judge of when that will be. Just remember that you're in a period of your life when you can benefit from a little self-indulgence, and that is a thought that can guide you and help you not to worry about the crazy foods you may be eating.

5

STRESS
AND ANXIETY ATTACKS

Dear Lynn,

My husband died eight months ago after a motorcycle accident. He suffered internal injuries and died in the hospital without regaining consciousness. I thought I had already been through the most searing pain possible and that I was past the worst of the grieving. But two months ago I started experiencing terrible anxiety attacks. I didn't know what was happening to me. I'd wake up in the middle of the night shaking, crying, afraid. I've never had nightmares in my life and have always been a sound sleeper, but now I find I'm even afraid to close my eyes. A few weeks ago, I was in the supermarket waiting at a check-out line when I started to shake for no reason. I had to leave my groceries and walk out of the store to breathe. I thought I was going to faint and my heart was beating like mad. I have a job as an office manager, and I make a decent living and don't have big money worries. But suddenly I find myself terrified that I won't have enough money to pay the bills. Last week I had to leave my desk at work and go to the ladies' room quaking and breathing hard as though someone was chasing me—of course, no one was.

I'm afraid that I can't handle anything anymore. If a little thing like buying groceries can set me off, what else will? There are times when I feel like things are out of control. I think about it and say, "This just isn't me," but it is.

Stress is a fact of life for everyone, widowed or not. But widows can get hit extra hard, and if you're unable to cope with stress, it can be very dangerous. Some medical professionals refer to it as the silent killer. That's a strong statement, but true. Stress is known to be a major contributor to the six leading causes of death: heart disease, cancer, accidents, suicide, liver problems, and lung ailments. Stress can zap your energy and damage your relationships with people, your physical and emotional health, your sense of purpose, your ability to make decisions, and more.

> I guess whatever age, state, or development a widow is at, she always lives with fears and doubts, with worries that something is wrong, with concern about all the decisions that need to be made, but sometimes I feel overwhelmed and unable to deal with the stress.

If widowhood brought you one problem to solve, you would probably take care of it and just go on with your life. But the death of your husband is not an isolated event that happens and then is over. It creates a ripple effect that touches every aspect of your world. You're not only dealing with being a woman alone, but perhaps with being a single parent, with a reduction of income and status, with social pressure to return your life to normal, and the list can go on and on. There's little in your life that's left untouched. The high-intensity stress that some widows face comes from dealing with a pile of problems that might look like tumbling dominoes. There isn't a single individual decision or situation to handle, but a complete life change.

When doctors talk about stress, they describe it as the body's reaction to daily emotional and physical demands. You know how it feels when stress starts to mount up—sort of like a taut rubber band just before snapping. Your body starts pumping adrenaline into the bloodstream and prepares itself for action. This is known as the "fight-or-flight" response. When the initial alarm has passed, the body relaxes and returns to its normal state. If your body doesn't have a chance to return to normal, but continues bouncing back to its snapping point, then exhaustion begins to set in. Your energy wears down; your body's resources are used up; stress hormones (adrenaline) are expended; and the whole body system starts to break down. That's basically how stress works. For many widows, it seems the body rarely has a chance to move out of its stressful state. That's when the real problems start. The idea is to get control of your stress before you reach that point.

I became very familiar with stress and, for me, the most appropriate and straightforward definition is "an exaggerated feeling of apprehension about the future." That's where most of my stress came from. I anticipated the future with dread, hopelessness, and helplessness. Whatever was going to happen, I just knew it would be awful.

Psychologists agree with that definition and go on to say that stress is caused by the feeling of not being in control of your life. They also say that change and unpredictability cause stress. As a widow, you understand those conclusions all too well.

I never thought positive things, such as success and challenge, were factors in stress. I only thought of it as a negative thing because that's what it's been for me. I have terrible headaches, and sometimes I have the go-to-bed-and-throw-up kind of stress and I'm totally whacked out for a couple of days. The smallest thing can set it off.

I can make a long list of the things that cause stress—everything from a broken shoelace to the threat of nuclear war—and widows face the normal, everyday causes with a lot of extras thrown in. I think that just as important as recognizing the causes of stress is knowing how to deal with them. Coping with stress is necessary if you want to maintain good physical and emotional health, and so this chapter addresses teaching you about one of the most powerful defenses you have against stress: learning how to relax.

Any information given here is not intended to take the place of your doctor's advice or treatment. If your feelings of stress seem more than you can handle—if you're drinking more than you should, taking drugs, suffering from severe health problems or phobias—you must consult your physician. Many of the suggestions given here might well be used along with professional medical advice.

LIVING ON A
TWENTY-FOUR-HOUR PLAN

Of all the stressful symptoms I've experienced, the ones that hit during the night were the worst. They occurred most often around four in the morning, when I would jolt awake, shuddering with sheer terror. I have never been so afraid in my life. My heart would pound; my skin would break out in a cold sweat; and I'd start to shake. I was sure I was going to die, and to tell the truth there were many nights I went to bed praying that I wouldn't wake up in the morning.

I feel haunted by fear and can't shake it. Every moment is filled with thoughts about what will I do, how can I get things in order again. Everything seems too much. Every decision weighs a ton. I don't feel I can take the stress anymore.

I have heard that the Scandinavians use a phrase meaning "hour of the wolf" to describe the early morning—between four and five—when our greatest fears drift up from the subconscious to haunt us like a ghostly wolf stalking its prey. Your hour of the wolf may strike at two in the afternoon when you're at work, at five in the morning, or at six at night as you stand on the supermarket check-out line. Wherever and whenever it happens, it is a painful and terrifying experience.

I used to get caught up in what I call the "what-if?" syndrome during my hour of the wolf:

What if I get sick or disabled?

What if I have a nervous breakdown?

What if I can't support my children?

What if I become a bag lady?

What if. . .what if. . .what if. . .

That's fear at work. The psychology of fear is the projection of negative feelings. As a widow, you probably can't conceive that the future has good things in store for you. For a long time I didn't either.

A friend who is a member of Alcoholics Anonymous (AA) persuaded me to try one of that organization's techniques, and I found it to be extremely effective. I understand now that recovery from alcoholism is in many ways similar to recovery from bereavement, and I've used other AA methods in my life.

AA teaches you to begin living on the twenty-four-hour plan. It is absolutely impossible to worry about tomorrow or next week if you live one day at a time—or one hour at a time. Over and over again, I would say to myself: "Stay in the present. There's nothing I can't handle in the next twenty-four hours." It is enormously comforting because it is always true.

Living your life in twenty-four-hour segments will help you avoid creating those terrifying what-if? scenarios in your head. Next week won't be such a worry if you stay in the present. I would also sit down and make a list of things I wanted to do in the next twenty-four hours—positive things like making a phone call about an overdrawn account at the bank or making sure my daughter had the new pair of sneakers she needed, or writing a letter that was overdue. I would try to accomplish something in that twenty-four-hour span, and when I did, it reminded me that I indeed had some control over my life.

Another way of combating stress is to use what I call the Tara Jar. Scarlett O'Hara of *Gone With the Wind* is a famous procrastinator, and it worked for her. Whenever a problem or situation became too painful, she'd put it on hold and say, "I'll think about that tomorrow." She usually came up with the right answer when she thought about it later at Tara, the family home. Not everyone has a southern plantation home like Tara, but you can keep a Tara Jar. I've used a Tara Jar and have introduced it to my widow groups with great success. Anything I wanted to think about tomorrow, I'd write down and put in the jar. By the time I got around to opening the jar, the problem usually would have resolved itself.

Get yourself a big, attractive jar and whenever life feels frightening or things just get to be too much, write your problem down on a piece of paper and put it in the Tara Jar. Writing it down seems to exorcise the stress demons.

I was hit with several severe forms of stress at the same time. I had terrible anxiety attacks with heart palpitations and a feeling that I would pass out. Or sometimes I'd be so afraid that I couldn't move.

PHYSICAL EXERCISE

My stationary exercise bicycle was my best friend during those early days and nights of widowhood. Whenever I felt anxious, I'd get on my bicycle and peddle away. I'd get there from underneath my covers in bed or from the kitchen, where I'd be making dinner, by using a slogan I made up for myself: MOVE YOUR BODY, MOVE YOUR BODY. No matter where I was at home or what I was doing, if anxiety came on hard, I'd MOVE YOUR BODY to my bicycle.

I'm not suggesting that you do an hour of aerobics. Weight loss and firm-up sessions are not the objective. Exercise is an excellent antidote to stress, and you don't have to set great demands on yourself to get results. You can use what I call the nibble method.

When I peddled the stationary bicycle, I would plan to do three or four revolutions. There's no way I could cop out of doing so few. I'd always do more than that, once I got started, and it *always* made me feel better. If you don't have a bicycle, run in place three times, or do three leg lifts, or jump rope twice, or swing your arms twice. The toughest part is getting started, but once you get your blood circulating you'll feel better and your exhaustion will begin to lift.

If this type of exercise isn't for you, try cleaning the house. I scrubbed every inch of bathroom tile—one tile at a time—with a toothbrush before I got the exercise bicycle. A widow from Baltimore told me that she saved the task of changing her bed sheets for the middle of the night, so that she would get up and do something during her hour of the wolf.

The point of it is that exercise—any kind of exercise—helps to alleviate anxiety. You'll find that the more you do, the more you *can* do. I summed this up with another of my slogans: Energy comes from exerting energy.

I had terrible anxiety attacks, but I thought it was just me. I was afraid to tell anyone. I was afraid they would say I was crazy and take my children away from me. When I'm in such a state my imagination tends to go wild.

THE QUIET MIND

There was a time in my life when I would pop a Valium whenever I felt stressed out. I stuffed my feelings down inside, and the Valium would help to keep them there. I was well on my way to developing a full-blown addiction. I had a Faustian bargain going—just one more pill, just one more pill—and I bargained myself right into a corner. My body built up a tolerance to the drug, and it wasn't long before I was walking around in a state of agitated depression, sort of an electrified numbness. I knew I had to find another way to deal with the stress.

I decided to give myself what turned out to be a valuable gift. I investigated various meditation techniques to find one that would work for me. I learned that you can control a lot of what you feel by practicing breathing exercises and meditation. *I had control over*

111

the way I felt. The answer was not in a pill bottle, but in the pit of my stomach. That was a major turning point for me. It didn't make my problems disappear, but it allowed me to calm myself and begin to deal with them.

Meditation is commonly used today in the treatment for anxiety. It might surprise you to know that many large corporations have established stress-management programs to help their employees cope. And hundreds of private stress-management centers have cropped up all over the country. Almost all of them teach some form of meditation.

At times my mind seems like a squirrel in a cage, going round and round trying to find a way out. The need for patience is tremendous. I am a person accustomed to organizing and planning, but each time I have to make a decision, it distresses me so. I have wanted so much to simply lie down and cut my wrists and let my life flow away and be at peace. What stops me is not fear of death, but the knowledge that I must remain here to hold things together for my family.

You might not think you're getting immediate results from meditation, but you are benefiting whether or not you notice it right away. The benefits are cumulative. The effects add up even if it feels like nothing is happening. You have to stay with it. Meditation is very easy to learn, it's definitely relaxing, and I recommend it because it has worked for me.

GETTING READY

In order to get the most out of meditation, it's important to eliminate possible interruptions. Take the phone off the hook. If it rings in the middle of your meditation time, it can be very disturbing. Put the cat or dog outside or in another room. If you have young children and they cannot be left untended, try meditation in the evening when they're asleep or during their nap time.

Have a blanket handy. A relaxed state can lower your body temperature, and you might feel chilled. If you have the time, a hot bath before meditation is wonderful.

If at any point during your meditation you feel you have to move—your leg falls asleep or you develop a maddening itch on your nose—go ahead and move. You're not a Zen master. It's much more distracting to force yourself *not* to relieve an itch than it is to just scratch and quietly go back to your meditation.

Don't set your alarm clock to wake you after twenty minutes, which is how long you should allow yourself. It will jolt you right out of your relaxed state, not to mention your skin. If you absolutely *have* to be up at a certain time, set a clock radio so that it will play soft music. It's fine if you fall asleep. You'll awaken refreshed and rested.

MEDITATION TECHNIQUE NUMBER ONE Lie down on the bed or floor or sit in a chair. Whatever spot you pick, put yourself in the most comfortable position for you.

Once you're in a comfortable position, breathe normally. Focus on your breathing— the sound of it, how it feels. Slowly inhale a little deeper through the nose and exhale a little more through the mouth. You should feel your breathing from the pit of your stomach. It might help to silently count: Inhale . . . one . . . two . . . three . . . and exhale . . . one . . . two . . . three . . . .

Continue to breathe slowly, and let your eyelids relax and feel heavy. Let the area all around your eyes feel relaxed. Feel your forehead and eyebrows relaxing. Then move up to the scalp and feel that relaxing. Let your cheeks go limp, and let your mouth drop open a little. If you have trouble *letting* this happen, just say in your mind, "My eyelids are relaxing. They feel heavy and relaxed. My cheeks are relaxed and limp." Eventually, you'll feel it.

Continue this process, moving down from your head to your neck, shoulders, back, stomach, chest, abdomen, upper legs, knees, lower legs, and eventually your feet.

Tell yourself that your ankles, toes, and heels are relaxed. Once you have relaxed your feet, I expect that you'll feel a difference—even if it's slight—in your sense of calm. With practice, you'll notice an even more drastic change and you'll also be able to run through these steps more quickly.

When you're relaxed in this manner, you can just sit in the silence for a few minutes listening to your quiet breathing. Or you can use some of the visualization suggestions in this chapter.

When you're ready to end your meditation, take a deep breath and gently stretch your arms and legs. Move your feet and wiggle your toes to get your circulation going.

MEDITATION TECHNIQUE NUMBER TWO

At Beth Israel Hospital in Boston and at the Harvard Medical School, a group of doctors conducted a joint research project to determine the effects of meditation as therapy in treating anxiety. After eight weeks, they found an overall improvement in 34 percent of the test subjects. The subjects' self-evaluations showed that 63 percent felt they had benefited from meditation. Here is the technique they used:

Sit quietly in a comfortable position.

Close your eyes.

Deeply relax all your muscles, beginning at your feet and progressing up to your face. Keep them deeply relaxed.

Breathe through your nose. Become aware of your breathing. As you breathe out, say the word "one" silently to yourself. For example, breathe in . . . out, "one"; in . . . out, "one."

Continue for twenty minutes. You may open your eyes to check the time, but do not use an alarm. When you finish, sit quietly for several minutes, at first with closed eyes and later with opened eyes.

Don't worry about whether you are successful in achieving a deep level of relaxation. Maintain a passive attitude and permit relaxation to occur at its own pace. When distracting thoughts occur, ignore them, and continue repeating "one." With practice, the response should come with little effort. Because the metabolic rate increases when you're digesting food and decreases during meditation, for best results wait two hours after any meal before meditating.

The differences between the two meditation techniques I've given are subtle, but try them both and see which is most effective for you.

I call my anxiety attacks AA's because they have become so familiar and common. I wake up in the middle of the night with AA's so severe I am unable to move.

VISUALIZATION FOR RELAXATION

Children know how to use their imagination to create a private world in which to play. They can put together a whole kingdom with castles, brave knights, white stallions, and a princess to be rescued. If you've ever watched children building a sand castle on the beach, you've seen how they drift off into a world of their own making, totally absorbed in the freedom of imagination.

The use of your imagination can be a positive tool for coping with stress, but many of us have forgotten how. I used to use my imagination a lot, except I would create the most horrendous scenes of poverty, illness, and loneliness. But I found that it's well worth the minimal effort it takes to remember how to use your imagination to your advantage.

Many medical professionals now acknowledge the effectiveness of visualization in promoting healing. There is still much to learn about the connection between the mind and body, but there is enough material available to know that there is in fact a connection, that the body and mind work as a team. I find the power of visualization an amazing way to relax myself in moments of stress; it even works as a method for preventing stress. The beauty of visualization is that you can use its techniques just about anywhere. They can be especially effective when used during meditation. These exercises are best done with your eyes closed.

VISUALIZATION EXERCISES

- Imagine a light bulb just above your head. Switch the bulb on. Feel yourself being showered with a beautiful and warm white light. Imagine this bright light cascading from the top of your head to your toes and washing away your stress. Keep the light on until everything feels washed away. When you're finished, simply turn off the light.

- Imagine you have a soft white blanket, and wrap it around yourself. Pretend that the blanket can absorb your stressful feelings like a sponge. Let the blanket take the stress from you. Then remove the blanket and shake it out, letting all the stress blow away from you. Shake it out until everything is gone. Fold it up and put it away for later use.

- Imagine a bunch of beautiful colored balloons with strings attached. Hold the strings in your hand, and pretend that each of the balloons carries your stress. Then release them and watch them float away from you. Keep watching them until they're out of sight, taking your stressful feelings away.

- Close your eyes and imagine there is a white door in front of you. Open the door and create a mental picture of a beautiful place—a garden, or a beach, or a peaceful lake. Now step through the door into the scene you have created. Think of the word "calm" and feel how soothing the sound of that word is. Allow yourself to smell the flowers or the salt air and to hear the sounds of birds, the ocean, and a soft breeze. Really let yourself *be there*. When you're finished, walk back through the door and close it behind you. It's always there to return to whenever you want.

- Imagine that you've wrapped your stress in a small box. Tie a string around it. Lift the box above your head. Now picture two hands reaching down to take the package away from you. Release the package and let it be taken away.

- Imagine a blank screen in front of you that looks like a television screen. Notice that it's full of little squiggles and doodles. The markings represent your stressful thoughts. Now make the screen go blank so it looks like your television when it's turned off. If any of the little squiggles come back, just push them aside by letting the screen go blank again.

I feel like a lost and terrified child who has been abandoned. I have anxiety attacks all the time, and when they occur I simply can't move. I feel frozen on the outside and all shaky on the inside.

THE BREATH OF LIFE

One of the most common responses to stress is that your breathing becomes very shallow. You tense up and start taking short breaths, reducing the flow of oxygen into your body at a time when you need it most. Your pulse rate goes up, your muscles tighten, and you feel like you're ready to flee for your life.

Oxygen is necessary for your body to perform properly. You need oxygen in order to change fuel (food) into energy, which is what your body runs on. A lack of oxygen can cause fatigue, confusion, sluggish feelings, and worst of all—panic. Inhaling brings oxygen into the body, and exhaling releases carbon dioxide and other waste that your body doesn't need. Breathing is easy. You've been doing it all your life! And learning to breathe in a way that reduces stress is easy, too.

BREATH-AWARENESS EXERCISE Lie down on the floor or on a bed. Pull up your knees, and put your feet firmly on the floor or mattress.

Take a moment to be aware of the way you're breathing.

Listen to the sound of your breathing.

Inhale easily through your nostrils. You don't need a champion breath. Just do it gently, letting your abdomen and then your chest rise; finally, as the lungs fill, you'll feel the breath just under your collarbone.

Exhale slowly through the mouth, letting the air out with an o-o-o sound. Pull in your abdomen and squeeze out more air. When you can't make the o-o-o sound anymore, let go. You will notice that your body easily takes in a deep breath to fill your lungs. Try exhaling again, the same way. By practicing this exercise, you will notice that your body will make you breathe automatically as soon as there is room in your lungs after exhaling.

For a quick, calming oxygen fix, take a deep breath through your mouth. Hold it. Say "Hold it" to yourself four times, so that you hold your breath for about seven seconds.

Let your breath out slowly.

As you let it out, think of a pleasant scene. You can use the one in the visualization exercises in this chapter. Keep the scene in your mind, and deliberately relax your muscles.

With practice, you can train yourself to do this exercise at your desk at work, in a waiting room, or anywhere you feel you need it.

ALTERNATE-NOSTRIL BREATHING
This exercise acts as a natural tranquilizer. I do it for at least three minutes whenever I feel extremely tense or nervous. It never fails to both calm and energize me.

Close off your right nostril by pressing your right thumb against it. Exhale slowly and evenly through your left nostril. Now inhale slowly through the same nostril.

With the pinkie of your right hand, block off your left nostril and release your thumb

123

from the right nostril. Exhale through the right nostril, and slowly inhale through the same nostril.

Repeat from the beginning. Continue alternating nostrils for three minutes (or until your nose feels clear). As you exhale each time, imagine fear and pain leaving your body.

EMERGENCY BREATHING If your stressful feelings build to the point of a panic attack and nothing seems to help, lie down on the floor and raise your knees to your chest. Let the floor hold you up. Breathe—inhale through your nose— . . . one . . . two . . . three . . . four . . . —and exhale through your nose— . . . one . . . two . . . three . . . four . . . . I used this exercise at night if things got really bad, and it always helped.

I have more or less gotten over my incessant paranoia about losing my job, but there are still many nights when I will suddenly wake up in a cold sweat convinced that (a) there is an intruder in the house who is going to kill me and my daughter, (b) my daughter has stopped breathing, (c) the boiler in the basement is going to blow up. You can fight against these things, but they seep into your unconscious like a poison gas.

TENSING AGAINST STRESS

In 1929, Dr. Edmond Jacobson developed a method of relaxing by tensing the body. It's still widely used today and considered very effective. His method is based on the idea that it is easier to tense muscles first and then feel the contrasting relaxation. Areas of the body are tensed, one at a time, and then released. However, if you have had any kind of recent injury, do not do this exercise until you have healed.

TENSING TECHNIQUE Lie down and make yourself comfortable. Close your eyes. Keep your arms at your sides, fingers open.

Put your toes together, pigeoned-toed, with your heels slightly apart. Push your toes down and away from you. That tightens your leg muscles. Tighten your thighs. Tighten your buttocks. Hold that tense feeling for about seven seconds and then release, relax. Feel the difference?

Then move on to the next area. Close

your fingers in a tight fist. Tense your wrists and lower and upper arms. Hold again for seven seconds and then release.

The next areas to focus on are the lower back, the chest, the stomach, and the abdomen. Concentrate on tensing these areas, hold for seven seconds, and let go.

Finally, concentrate on the shoulders, neck, face, and head. Clench your teeth together and tightly close your eyes. Tense your shoulders and neck; hold for seven seconds and then relax.

You can really feel this exercise as you move from area to area.

At the moment, I am a long way from being a well-adjusted widow, and although I try to live a day at a time, the trying is easier than the doing, to put it mildly. At age forty, I feel as I did when I attended summer camp, then college years later. "Homesick" is the only word I can attach to this feeling, and this time it stays with me. I think that trying to project my life for the years ahead distresses me as much as anything right now.

WHAT YOU EAT

If you use the stress-reduction suggestions in this chapter and then have a cup of coffee during your next stress attack, you're working at cross-purposes. The caffeine in coffee will not help you relax. Besides coffee, chocolate and many soft drinks contain caffeine. None of these will help when you feel stressed out. For some, it is an impossible suggestion to eliminate coffee altogether, but when you feel stress, at least cut down your caffeine intake.

The first thing many people do during a stressful time is pour themselves an alcoholic beverage. Alcohol is a depressant, but the sugar content of alcohol can pick you up and then drop you flat. You may already feel like you're on an emotional roller coaster, and alcohol won't make it any easier.

Sugar in general is something to watch out for and avoid. Also check for salt in the ingredients of packaged foods, and eliminate salt in cooking.

Do eat more less-stress foods, such as:

Asparagus

Brown rice

Cabbage

Corn

Squash

Yams

Vitamin C supplement or foods containing vitamin C

I am trying to take one day at a time, but it seems when I take a step forward I end up falling back two.

AFFIRMATIONS

I have learned that words have an enormous effect on the mind, and if you give yourself positive suggestions, they can change the way you feel. It's as though the mind is a big, dumb computer that will put out whatever you put in.

When I suffered from intense psychic pain, it helped me to know that a human being cannot possibly sustain such terrible stress forever. I'd say to myself, "It will pass, it will pass, it will pass." And eventually it *did* pass.

The sound of a word can be soothing, especially if it paints a pleasant picture in your mind; "ocean" and "home" are examples. Try repeating one of these words again and again. It doesn't take long to feel the effects.

Over the years, I have gathered many key words and phrases to use during moments of anxiety and also to lessen and even prevent stress attacks. Try repeating the words "I am calm," and see for yourself how powerful saying them aloud can be.

Some affirmations are like prayers. It doesn't matter whether or not you consider yourself a religious person or if you're a member of a church or have a religious affiliation. A quiet moment spent reciting an affirmation or prayer can leave you feeling quite peaceful. There is one that I particularly like. It was written in 1934 by the Protestant theologian Reinhold Niebuhr. The United Service Organizations (USO) distributed millions of copies of it to servicemen during World War II, and it was adopted as the motto of Alcoholics Anonymous:

God grant me the serenity to accept

the things I cannot change,
courage to change the things I can,
and the wisdom to know the difference.

It's also important to focus on the now, instead of yesterday or tomorrow. Here's an affirmation for just that—living in the moment:

> I am willing
> to let each moment I experience
> be the *only* moment
> getting my attention.

I discovered the Ninety-first Psalm after a widow from Illinois suggested that I look it up in my Bible. "I always turn to it when I feel lonely and fearful," she wrote.

> He is my refuge and my fortress:
> My God; in him will I trust . . .
> Thou shalt not be afraid for the terror
>   by night;
> Nor for the arrow that flieth by
>   day;
> Nor for the pestilence that walketh in
>   darkness;
> Nor for the destruction that wasteth at
>   noonday. . . .

There shall no evil befall thee. . . .
For he shall give his angels charge over
   thee,
To keep thee in all thy ways.

6

HELP FROM DREAMS

Dear Lynn,

I hesitate to use such a familiar greeting to someone I've never met, but I think of you as a good friend.

My husband died last year. I've loved him since I was seventeen, and it was a magical time, all fifteen years of our marriage. I didn't work except for eight years. I owned my own clothing shop. Most of my life was spent as a wife and mother, which I enjoyed. We had one child, and we both adored her and took equal responsibility to raise her. When she left for college just recently, I really suffered from the empty-nest syndrome, and I'm lonely now in this house all by myself. I'll probably sell it soon and move into something smaller. I've never heard anyone talk about the way widows dream about their husbands. Anyway, I started having the same dream again and again.

In the dream, he's standing on a river-bank, and I am across from him on the other side. He just stands there and sometimes waves to me. I keep hollering for him to hurry up or we'll be late (I don't know for what). He just stands there and finally turns around and walks away. It was a Saturday when my hus-band died. He was waiting for me to play golf. He was in the garage rearranging his tools when he had a heart attack and died. I never had a chance to say good-bye to him. This has always bothered me. The dreams don't frighten me, but I wonder if they have anything to do with this.

Here is one of the recurring dreams I had about Martin: We are in the south of France, and Martin and I are in the water. The sun is just starting to go down. I am holding on to a little piece of wood with a stick stuck into it, and I'm floating around in the ocean. Martin is off in the background, a distance from me. I can see him. He's talking to a man I don't recognize.

I yell to Martin, "Let's go. We better go back now. It's getting dark and I can't swim. I don't like being out in the water like this."

"I'm not going back with you," he says.

"I can't go on alone," I yell. "I'll never find my way."

"You're going to have to. I can't go back."

It was such a clear dream, so real, that sometimes I'd wake up expecting to find myself floating around in the ocean. There were mornings I would be glad just to have had a glimpse of Martin, to have spent a moment feeling he was real flesh and blood. There were also mornings I'd wake up feeling cheated, angry that he had left me all over again, and more alone than ever. It was torture to be so close to him and not be able to convince him to come back with me.

I thought I was the only one who had dreams like this. For a long time, I was very reluctant to talk about the nighttime meeting ground Martin and I shared. I felt it would sound as if I wasn't quite glued together. But when I was preparing the material that became *Widow*, I spent a lot of time reviewing the journals I had kept, and among those pages I discovered a record of some of my dreams, not that I could have forgotten them if I wanted to. They had a very dramatic effect on me.

I didn't do anything with the dreams then. Eventually, they occurred with less and less frequency, and I didn't pay as much attention to them. I realize now that as I slowly worked my way through my grief I changed, and so did the content of my dreams. Quite a few years after *Widow* was published, I still hadn't done much talking about dreams, but I was counseling a young widow who brought up the subject. She started to tell me about one of her dreams. "We were in a couple of those little-kid boat rides you see at carnivals," she said. "He was in a blue boat, and I was in a different one. I think mine was red. I don't know why we weren't together. It was night, but the place was all lit up the way carnivals are, and we were having a terrific time. All of a sudden the lights started to dim just as though someone had slowly been pulling on a dimmer switch. I turned to ask my husband what he thought was happening and say that maybe we should take the boats in and go get some dinner, when I noticed he had drifted way off, practically across the lake. I called to him, but all he did was wave and keep going."

She wasn't frightened by the dream, but it affected her in the same mixed-up way mine had. She was angry and sad and happy all at the same time. She wanted to know what I thought of it.

I didn't know what to say. Although I'd been interested in dreams, I felt it was a little out of my league to be interpreting hers. I agree with Dr. Montague Ullman, author of *Working with Dreams* (Jeremy Tarcher, Inc., 1985), who says that the person who has the dream is the only real expert on its meaning, so I really didn't feel comfortable analyzing her dream. But I did notice the obvious similarity to my own swimming dream—the light being dimmed, Martin not returning with me—and told her so. And, hoping that it would help, I told her what my dreams meant to me personally. I feel they had some important role in my accepting Martin's death as final. I felt that they were a private, quiet way for me to acknowledge that Martin was gone, dead, and would not be coming back.

The explanation was right for me, and she seemed to find some comfort in it. I was really stretching into the bereavement process in a way I never had before, but I felt it was no accident that my dreams, in some odd, almost jumbled way, revealed feelings I had barely begun to admit to myself. Over the years, I've tried to keep an open mind about what all this means and of what value it can be. I've now spent many hours discussing this subject with widows and medical professionals. And then I have my own dreams to consider. More than anything else, they have confirmed for me that our dreams are worth paying attention to.

There is no material compensation for the loss of energy that is embodied in the human being. It was injected into every facet of my life. Even into my dreams after his death.

DREAM LIFE

No one really knows where our dreams come from or even why we dream, and I'm not taking on the task of trying to figure it out in this chapter. I'll leave that for the researchers, who are better equipped to push behind the dreams and find the answers to where, why, and how. My interest in this comes from discovering, through my own dream life, that there is very definitely some connection between what goes on there and what goes on in my waking life. My concern in this chapter is to make widows aware of the resources we all have to help us cope with grief and to find ways to reach acceptance and allow our lives to go on. If my personal experience can be an indicator of what our dreams can teach us about ourselves, then I can state with confidence that we have in our grasp a powerful healing tool.

No matter what state of mind you present to the outside world, our dreams don't lie. We're honest in our dreams. I think it's because when we're asleep the defense system we use to protect our grieving selves doesn't exist in the same way it does when we're awake. With the defenses down, we are free to express our feelings through a scenario that is perhaps full of symbolism and metaphor but that has an underlining of truth. Maybe that's the key to what makes dreams valuable to us. They can tell us things about how we feel—where we are in the grief process—that are not as clear or unprotected when we're awake. I think that they allow us to freely deal with certain aspects of grief and that the content of our dreams is in direct response to that need.

I've noticed that three basic themes seem to repeat themselves in dreams that concern bereavement. They are searching, abandonment, and letting go. Certainly, there are others, but these are the ones that stand out for me, and so I think they're the best illustration of some of the ways in which we express the emotions of grief through dreams. I am not asking you to take the meanings I've found in my dreams and apply them to your own. I only want you to begin to consider your dreams in a way you may never have before. Keep in mind that just as there's no timetable for the stages of grief widows experience, there is none that I can point to for our dreams. There's no "six-month-widow's dream" or "one-year-after-the-death dream." They can appear at any time during bereavement, and their message is unique to each widow's individual experience.

I want to address each of the dream themes separately and tell you the way in which they were played out in my dreams of Martin and how they provided insight into some of the feelings and fears I faced in accepting his death. My dreams didn't solve all of my problems, and I want to be very clear about that. Finding my way through grief to acceptance required hard work, and because I didn't have the benefit of the information and self-help groups that are available to you today, it took me a long and difficult time. But in addition to all the other resources you may be utilizing, I encourage you to take a look at your dreams, and perhaps they will provide you with yet another way to heal and understand yourself. If you're in a widows' counseling group or working with a medical professional, you might want to introduce the subject of dreams. Or you may just keep a journal of your dreams yourself. Either way, I hope you will begin to consider your dream life as another practical tool that can provide insight and release and assist you in many ways toward recovery.

I feel funny talking about my dreams. I mean, my husband is more alive in them than he was when he was alive. It's a strange experience. There are many mornings I wake up very sad, but sometimes I expect to open my eyes and see him lying beside me.

SEARCHING

Here is another one of my dreams: I am walking out of the building in which I live into the streets of New York City. It's dark and chilly, and the city has a strange quality to it. I don't feel any familiarity with the streets or buildings or the surroundings that are in my neighborhood. I am carefully walking down streets and around corners, poking into alleys and doorways looking for something I can't seem to find anywhere. I begin to hurry, knowing that if I can just find that one thing (in the dream I don't know what "the thing" is), then I can go home in peace.

I would usually wake up from this dream feeling that something was left unfinished. I'd be uncomfortable and sort of empty. I don't think it's difficult to figure out what I was searching for—Martin, of course—or that I wouldn't be able to find it. I don't think I had yet reached a point where I could acknowledge *what* had been lost. Knowing Martin was dead didn't stop me from looking for "it." Many young children have similar responses. Maybe it's because their defense mechanisms aren't firmly in place the way those of adults are. Some children respond to the news of death by suggesting that everyone should go out and look for Dad, and I think I was playing out something very similar to that in my dreams.

Many widows have searching dreams soon after their husbands have died. We know that a death has occurred, of course. We have a death certificate, a funeral or memorial service, and condolence cards to help us remember. But for a time, some things are too painful to think about and accept, so perhaps we disguise them the way I did in my dream. I think I reduced the problem to something I *could* handle—if something is lost, I will go out and find it. There's no doubt about it: My searching dreams very definitely correlated to the way I was feeling, and that had to do with denying the fact that Martin was dead. The way your dream is set up can be very different from mine. It can appear as a maze instead of streets or a building for which there is no entrance or no key to the entrance. Or *you* may be what's lost in the dream. The message, to me, is the same. This kind of dream frequently appears at the point before the widow acknowledges that the lost object, the person, is not to be found. From here, my dreams took a turn. Instead of searching and not finding, I was able to find but not have. It was an interesting step forward.

I was so happy when I would dream about him and so sad when I woke up. Sometimes I wished I could just live in my dreams.

ABANDONMENT

When Martin died and my children and I were left to fend for ourselves, without money and without knowing how to survive alone, I felt we had been deserted. I was furious with him for dying. Yes, I thought he had abandoned us, and at times I hated him for it. This, too, showed up in my dreams. Here's one of those: Martin and I are at a large party, but we've become separated in the crowd. I'm wandering around looking for him and finally spot him across the room. But there's something wrong with the picture before me. Martin is *with* another woman! As I walk across the room my anger builds. She's tall and pretty. Martin is standing so close to her, and they're laughing. I walk up to him demanding to know what's going on.

"Who is this woman?" I say.

The woman responds, "You had your chance with him. He's mine now. He's not coming back with you."

"What about the children?" I say.

"You'll have to take care of them yourself," she says.

Martin never says a word.

The dream reminds me of the end of one of my favorite films, *Gone With the Wind*. Rhett Butler has walked out on Scarlett O'Hara, and she tells herself, "There must be some way I can get him back." For me, the dream means just that. If Martin is gone, but has only left me for another woman, then there is hope. Certainly I can find a way to get him back.

A lot of widows dream this, and I think in my own dream the other woman represents death on a certain level. In my inability to accept Martin's death, my dream transforms his leaving into abandonment. If Martin is dead, the problem cannot be solved. If he has left me for another woman, perhaps it can be.

Other widows have told me of similar dreams with a slightly different twist. They can see their husband, but somehow can't get to him. There may be a glass barrier between them. Or they may find themselves in a foreign place with a strange climate, not knowing the language or customs and unable to communicate with their husband. They can't get the message across —"Come home with me. Come back."— but they can see him and stand in front of him.

In this theme of abandonment, women actually experience happier dreams. Widows have told me that they find themselves interacting with their husbands in their dreams and everything appears quite normal. The family may be sitting down for dinner and the feelings are of love and warmth and safety, but somehow the dream always turns to a point where things aren't quite right. A friend of mine who is a widow told me this dream: "There was a lot of excitement and a feeling of fun in the house. We were all preparing, packing, and getting things in order to go away on vacation. We have three young children and live in a large home that is always full of noise and activity and some amount of disorganization. We used to spend every summer in a rented house on the New England shore. My husband would be able to spend a few weeks with us, but otherwise had to travel back and forth to his office and be with us only for weekends. It was a lot of work to move the entire household, and frequently Dan and I would get on each other's nerves. Nothing serious, but stressful. As I said, in the dream, everything was going so perfectly, so happily, that I stopped to wonder about it. I thought it was a little odd, almost too good to be true. At that point in the dream, my husband walked over to me and kissed me on the cheek and said, 'Well, I'll be off now.'

" 'What do you mean?' I said.

" 'I'll be going on alone,' he replied. And

with that he turned around and walked out the front door.

"I remember thinking in the dream that it was OK. He was probably just leaving early and would meet us at the vacation house."

There isn't another woman in this dream, but there appears to be another priority. Her husband is leaving, perhaps just going on ahead. Her feeling was that something wasn't exactly right, but that it could still be re-solved. The dream has the element of saying good-bye, but it's incomplete.

I have to be honest and say that these kinds of dreams were a little eerie for me. I really didn't feel that I would be OK without Martin, and in the dreams I held on to the hope that things would work out. But since the dream was mine and I set it up the way I did, part of me must have felt ready to move on, even though it was with great trepida-tion. There must have been, although I wasn't consciously aware of it, some sense of knowing that I could do it. Nobody had the dream but me. I was no longer searching, but finding, and I still couldn't have what I wanted.

If all this sounds a little crazy, I want to say again that although the dreams reflected

my emotional state when I was awake and
going about my business, raising my children, and holding a job, I was obviously
shifting and sorting out my situation by setting my dream stage in a certain way and
filling it with a cast of characters and a story
that allowed me to play out what I was feeling. I wasn't running around New York City
streets hunting for Martin during the day,
although I've talked about how I followed
men who looked like him. Maybe that's one
of the connections to the searching dream.
And finding him at the party was perhaps
the beginning of consciously acknowledging
that I would somehow have to go on alone. I
never woke up from the dream thinking,
"Aha, so that's where he is. With another
woman." I knew they were *dreams* and not
real physical situations. I came to understand
only later that they revealed my not wanting to accept death. It was too much. I
couldn't deal with an "end" in the dream,
and so I set my stage and story to reflect a
way out.

He kept telling me in my dreams to get
on with my life and to stop waiting for
him. I had to laugh a little. He was al-

ways so impatient. That's exactly what he would have said to me.

LETTING GO

The dreams that followed the "other woman" were like the one I opened this chapter with. They didn't give me an out. There was no other woman to win him back from. Instead, I was floating in an ocean, uncharted sea, if you will, and Martin was telling me directly that I would have to work it out myself—literally, sink or swim. There is the loss and the good-bye and on some level acknowledgment that I could make it on my own. Another woman friend of mine who is a widow told me this dream of loss and letting go: "In my dream, I was in San Francisco on business and on my way to a meeting. I found myself on a cable car. I had a lot on my mind and was at a critical crossroad in my life. I was facing an important decision about starting my own company and leaving the safety and support of a large, corporate environment. In the dream, I sat down in the cable car, deep in thought about my future. I was thinking how much I missed my husband's counsel and wisdom when I realized he was sitting next to me. I was so happy to see him and picked up the conversation—telling him about all the things that were happening—just as I would if we were sitting at home. I told him about my doubts and fears and that I was so happy that now we could do it together. 'No,' he said, 'it's up to you now. Go ahead and do it. It will work out fine, but I can't be with you. You have to do it for yourself.'

"With that, he started to get up and move toward the door. I was glued to my seat. I just couldn't seem to get myself up to follow him, and I yelled after him. He just kept going. At the last moment, he turned back to me and said, 'Don't be afraid. You'll be OK.' He waved and then was gone."

Powerful stuff. This friend told me that she woke up from the dream feeling very sad. But she made the decision to start her own business, and it worked out well for her. In a later conversation we had she said, "It was a very complex time of my life, but leaving the large company I had worked for and going out on my own was in fact a way of leaving the old me behind. It allowed me to shed an old identity and realize strength and talent on my own. I had no big company to fall back on, and I had no husband to support the decision. It was me, alone. I don't think it was a coincidence that finally accepting his death came at the same time I made this important decision to stand on my own two feet. As frightening as it all was, I felt more whole, stronger for it. I felt I was fulfilling more of who I could be, realizing potential and all that. Yes, the dream was a sad experience. In a way, I think my husband may have been reaching over from wherever he is to tell me to get on with it. The information came through in a dream, but I believe it was from him. I took a while to digest all of this. It didn't happen overnight. In fact, the same or similar dream was repeated a number of times, maybe until I got from it what I needed. But I look back at them as signaling a real turning point."

My friend found release in her dreams and confirmation of her growing acceptance of her husband's death and of being a woman alone who was able to cope. And maybe her husband really was sending information to her through the dream. Who can say for sure? I think the more important point is that she was ready to let go, and the dream helped her to do that.

We can look within and without for help. Within, our dreams sharpen the images of our stress until our emotions become defined. Within, our dreams gather together old and new responses to our problems. Some responses, outdated and inhibiting change, need to be discarded; others may, with refinement or repetition, generate change.[*]

Generating change is what is necessary to finally transform our sadness into joy, and loss into acceptance. Dreams don't take away grief, but I think they offer us an opportunity to look at where we are in the life crisis that is widowhood and to do so with clarity and a sense of safety.

Dreams have taken on a new and deeper importance for me because I've gained so much from them. Recognizing that something may be going on in our dreams that is directly related to the grief process may indeed offer us a unique way to heal emotionally. We can and should look around us for professional counseling and the support system that a widows' group can give, but within that framework we shouldn't dismiss the

[*]*The Variety of Dream Experience*, eds. Montague Ullman and Claire Limmer (New York: The Continuum Publishing Co., 1987).

wealth of information that may come into our understanding through dreams. I, for one, plan to pay closer attention to them from now on. I hope you will, too.

7

CHILDREN AND GRIEF

Dear Mrs. Caine,

I am fifteen years of age, and when my father died I was only just about eight years old. My father died of a heart attack. I don't know very much about it since my mother doesn't talk about it. But I have learned that my father had heart trouble for years. He died fast, I think. If I meet a new person who doesn't know about my dad, I'm always embarrassed to tell them. I feel they will treat me differently and pity me. I remember once in third grade we were talking about death and the teacher asked if anyone knew of another in the room who had lost a close relative. Someone mentioned that my dad had died. Would you believe it, at that point I didn't know what he died of! I didn't know what to say in the class. I wish my mom had explained it all to me. I didn't go to the funeral, but I know where my dad is buried. I'd like to go there and visit. I'd like to say a prayer or something, but I'll never be able to tell her about it.

Why is it that people don't tell me anything? Is this the way it always is? I don't have any experience, so I don't know. I still sometimes have nightmares that everyone is dead except me. I can't talk to any one, and that's why I'm writing this letter.

Consider this: Whatever you are feeling, your children—in their own way—are feeling, too. If you really think about that statement, you have some idea of what your child may be going through. Shock, anger, guilt, fear, and all the other emotions surrounding death are experienced by the children of widows. You have lost your husband. Your child has lost Dad. Each of you had a special relationship that has come to an end. For many widows, the first instinct is to protect their children from the unhappiness, the unpleasant details, the death. Others can't face it themselves, and so they have great difficulty helping their children to understand. If you shield your child from the reality of what has happened and is happening, you're not allowing the grief process to run its course. The kids can't take away your pain any more than you can take away theirs, but each of you must be given the resources that will help you work through grief to acceptance.

I have a little girl, five years old. She was four when her father died. I could not tell her until she asked me about two weeks later where her daddy was. She thinks he will get on an airplane in heaven and come home when he wants to. How do I explain that he won't? I wonder if her ideas will harm her in any way when she gets older?

FACING DEATH

Your child's reaction to death is directly related to your reaction to death. If your child sees that you don't communicate how you really feel, he or she probably won't either. Children know when something is wrong. If you try to hide it, you're sending contradictory signals. They'll suspect that things are pretty bad if you won't even talk about it or if you're smiling and being strong when they know that something disastrous has happened. If you close them out, they'll come up with all kinds of misinformation about what's going on. And as word filters around the neighborhood and school yard, they'll probably hear things from others. You'll agree that's not the best way for a child to learn about an important subject like death. A widow who attended one of my seminars gave me a powerful example of that. Her husband had committed suicide when she and her daughter were visiting a relative. "My husband shot himself," she told me. "I had no idea that he was thinking of doing it. We lived in a small town then, and no one would let their children come over and play with my daughter after her father died. One girl in her class at school said that she could never play with her again because her mother said our house had a ghost. For a long time, my daughter couldn't sleep at night."

Imagine someone putting an idea like that in *your* child's mind! Of course, some people are just idiots, but more and more we're isolated from death, and it has caused a lot of fear. There was a time when people died at home, when death and dying were part of the experience of the entire family, but no more. Now most people die in nursing homes or hospitals, and we're increasingly separated from that part of life. The result is that we and our children are very uncomfortable with death.

The fact is that over one million children lose one or both their parents to death by the age of fifteen. That alone is a good enough reason to educate our children better. Your children probably pick up a lot of ideas about death from television. They may see a cartoon in which a cat explodes in one scene and returns to go on with a new adventure in the next. That has to register some odd impressions about death. Other children learn through the death of a house pet. That experience can be a wonderful teacher, for many reasons. But what happens when the deceased pet is immediately replaced with another? Maybe the child is distracted from the loss and never grieves for his animal friend, and death never becomes final in his mind. Under these kinds of circumstances, you can understand how children develop distorted ideas about death.

You are an adult and probably have experienced the death of a friend or relative. Chances are you've been to a funeral before. None of those things paves the way for an easy widowhood, but they are experiences

157

most children—depending on the age group —don't have. And so it is up to you to provide a supportive atmosphere in which your child can grieve.

Without a doubt, the most crushing blow I was dealt was by my third-grade teacher. When the class was making Father's Day cards, she wouldn't allow me to make one for my brother or uncle because they were not my father. The kids in class picked up on it and started to ridicule me. She sent me to the lavatory until art period ended. I can now look back and realize how ignorant she was, but at the time it was a real trauma.

WHAT YOUR CHILD COMPREHENDS

It's important that you keep in mind your child's level of understanding and maturity when you talk about death. You wouldn't deal with a four-year-old child in the same way you would discuss death with a twelve-year-old. Psychologists have studied children's concept of death and dying and classify that understanding according to age and stage of development:

Birth to four years: Toddlers from twelve months on have what is described as a "sensory reaction" to the absence of their father. They're aware of the loss, but have no concept of what death is.

Ages five through nine: At this age, children become aware of the difference between life and death, but through "fantasy reasoning" often attribute death to some magical power that has taken their father.

Ages eight through twelve: By this time children have developed "factual reasoning." They understand the real cause of their father's death, but it remains a distant phenomenon that has no bearing on their own mortality.

Ages thirteen through eighteen: At this point in their cognitive development, kids have achieved "abstract reasoning" and fully understand the universality of death, including their own.

This information is a loose guideline, but if there's any firm rule to follow, it's that you must know your own children. You must observe them and listen to them and be aware of whether or not they comprehend what you tell them. It's possible that a four-year-old can understand death more easily than a six-year-old, or a seven-year-old more easily than a nine-year-old. I haven't categorized specific suggestions by age group because I don't think you should get locked into thinking that if your child is seven, he's automatically going to have to work through "fantasy reasoning." The age-group designations can overlap, so *you*—with the input of your child and the information that follows—must decide the best way to proceed.

I have been widowed for eight years. I just found out how much my twenty-one-year-old is still bothered by his father's death, and how much I wish I had gotten help for him sooner.

HELPING YOUR CHILD TO UNDERSTAND

Universally, no one disagrees that you must deal honestly with your child about death, and the sooner the better.

It may be days or weeks before the question of "Where's Dad?" comes up. Don't wait for questions from your child. Approach the subject as soon as you know that death is imminent or as soon as possible after a sudden death, and with a number of things in mind.

- You should be the one to speak to your child. Don't rely on a relative or friend to break the news. Your child is closer to you than anyone else, and is more likely to believe you and find comfort in your presence.

- Before you begin any discussion, think about what you want to say. You're upset, too, and not thinking all that clearly, so it's important to prepare ahead of time. Your child will remember and trust what you say, so consider before you speak.

- If you cry, your child may be frightened at first, but in order to know that sadness and tears are normal, it's OK for you to show emotion. But keep in mind that your child is not your confidant, and you shouldn't unburden yourself on him. If your own emotions are overpowering, you may need to vent your more intense feelings in another environment.

- Follow up the first discussion, and allow quiet time for additional questions.

161

One group of questions may be replaced with another as your child considers your initial explanations or needs further clarification.

Martin and I sat down with our children and explained that their Daddy had a serious grown-up's disease called cancer, but that the doctors were working hard to make him better. We thought we had done a wonderful job telling them because we were so honest. We did OK as far as we went, but it wasn't enough. Fourteen months later, I found out how ineffective we were when the hospital called to tell me that Martin had died. My son, Jonny, answered the phone and said, "It's the hospital, Mom. Maybe Daddy is *cured*." Obviously, we hadn't gotten through to him.

- Be aware of your child's reactions, and offer physical and emotional reassurance as necessary. For a child coming to grips with the death of his father, it seems like the world can never be the secure place it once was. Being physically close by touching, holding hands, and hugging helps a child feel safe.

- If at all possible, avoid sudden changes immediately following the death. A major move—new home, new school—may be too much for your child to handle. There is enough to deal with for now without losing friends and familiar surroundings.

- Notify the school or any organization your child belongs to, so that those in charge will be aware that a little extra attention may be needed.

- Your child may be asked inappropriate questions from outside the family. Words like "So, is you're mother dating anyone?" can have a devastating effect. Children often don't know how to respond to rude comments. Explain that they should reply, "You'll have to ask my mother," to any questions they feel uncomfortable handling.

- Remember that any untruth you tell your child will have to be unlearned later. I received a lesson in that from my daughter, Elizabeth, who was only five years old at the time. Our family cat, Kubla, was very ill, and the vet was unable to save him. Moments after I had privately given my permission, the doctor came out to tell us that the cat had been put to sleep. Elizabeth wanted to see him, and when the doctor arrived with Kubla she was furious. "You liar," she yelled at him. "That cat isn't asleep, he's dead. You killed my cat." She knew the difference and wouldn't accept anything but the literal truth.

My son keeps asking why his daddy died on his sixth birthday. I was at a loss so I told him that Daddy was celebrating just the same in heaven. Did I say the wrong thing?

QUESTIONS AND ANSWERS

There are three important questions to deal with first:

What is death?

Your child should understand that when a person is dead he will not return, that death is final. Death means that the person no longer eats, sleeps, or goes to work, that he is buried or cremated and won't be back. If there is an example of a family pet who has died, that's a good place to begin. If you have religious or philosophical beliefs about death, you may want to share them, but be sensitive about the way you present them.

Why do people die?

Explain the cause of death with honesty. If it was an illness, say so, but also help your child understand that it was very serious. "Daddy was sick and died" isn't enough. In a child's mind, there is little or no difference between a stomachache illness, common-cold illness, and your husband's cause of death. The next time you're sick in bed, your child may think that you will die, too. "Your father was in an accident, and we lost him" can translate for a child into a simple solution, "Well, why don't we go out and find him?" I remember that a guest in my home told me that her mother had passed away. Jon overheard her and later asked, "What does passed away mean?" I told him it meant that someone had died. He responded, "Well why didn't she say 'died,' if that was what she meant?" Avoid euphemisms when explaining death. Children will take what you say literally. Choose your words carefully. Keep it realistic and rational.

Where do dead people go?

There are good reasons why you should

think things out beforehand, and this is one of them. Listen to this explanation: "The angels took Daddy to live with God, and Daddy is happy there."

That doesn't sound too bad, but from a child's perspective it can send out a lot of wrong messages. If Dad "*lives* with God," then he's not dead. There is a logic to that. "The angels took Daddy" sounds like he was abducted, kidnapped. If the angels work for God and are good, then they'll bring Dad back. "Daddy is happy there." If *he's* so happy, why is everyone crying?

I lost my husband a couple of weeks ago. I am thirty-four years old, have two small children, and am expecting a third. I haven't a clue as to how I'm going to explain all this to them. I tell you, I don't think I can handle it.

FIRST REACTIONS

Your children will be affected by shock and numbness as an initial response, just as you are. It may feel strange explaining that Daddy is dead and having your child react in a very nonchalant manner. You may wonder if you've been heard or understood and may—

166

hours or days later—have to review the entire episode as though it's the first time. Your child may ask, even after a thorough explanation, when Dad will be coming home. Will he be there for the school play? When is he going to get the bicycle Dad promised? You must be prepared to patiently and carefully go through the events again. The finality of death is tough for you to accept; for a child it can be even more difficult. A child's universe has been built around his parents, and with death that universe is badly shaken. One of the things that can help your child is being part of the rituals that follow death.

My children all reacted differently at the funeral. Jamie screamed hysterically and had to leave. Todd didn't make a sound. Alex just held my hand and kept his eyes closed most of the time. It wasn't easy on them, but I'm glad they were there. I don't think any of them really believed their father was dead until then.

EVENTS SURROUNDING DEATH

Children should be included in the memorial service, the funeral, and postfuneral gatherings. It gives them the opportunity to mourn and to observe and communicate with others who grieve. You must explain the purpose of the funeral and exactly what will take place; that friends and family will be there and that some people might cry. I remember my son, Jon, saying, "I'll go to the funeral as long as you don't do anything spooky." I knew what he meant. He didn't want to see a dead person. Although I felt that seeing Martin would have helped Jon to accept the fact that his father was dead, the effect Martin's illness had on his appearance made the decision for me. We had a closed coffin and no "spooky" stuff.

If you do your job with care and with specific explanations, children will be less likely to be afraid of being there. When children see others mourning, they know that it's normal. If they attend the funeral or memorial service or both, someone should be available in case they want to leave, and they should know that it's OK to do so. Don't exclude children because you think they're too young. Check with your family doctor if you're uncertain about it. Being physically close to you during this time usually makes children feel more secure. Isolation from the events surrounding death breeds fear and fantasy and does not help the bereavement process. One widow wrote me that after her husband's funeral, friends came back to the house. She had explained the funeral to her son, but never thought to mention the reason people would be in the house afterward. She wrote, "When our friends arrived, he ran out of the living room in disgust yelling, 'Dad is dead, why are we having a party?' " If you tell children in detail and in advance what will happen and why, they probably won't have this kind of response.

The funeral may make death more real to your child, but grief doesn't end there. The shock of loss can alarm a child to a much greater degree than you, as an adult, can imagine. One of your child's protectors and safe-keepers is gone. When death and its implications begin to sink in, your child's most inner fear of who will now take care of him or her may surface.

My son, Jon, like many children, was told by ignorant but well-intentioned people that he was now the man of the family and that it was his responsibility to take care of *me*. One night I came home from work, and there was my nine-year-old son sitting at the head of the table. I asked him what he was doing in my chair. "Frank said that now I'm the man of the family," he responded, "and so I have to sit at the head of the table." I just looked at him, and somehow I found the right words. I said, "Jon, you're a big boy. You're a strong boy, and I love you a lot. But you're a boy. You're not a man. I am the head of the family. I am taking care of us, so get the hell back in your place." I could see the relief rolling off of him as I sent him back to his chair. It was as though a weight had been lifted from his shoulders.

Children must know that you are capable of taking charge of the family now. It's a larger responsibility than you counted on, but it is yours to deal with in the most positive way you can. By providing the security of your presence and the knowledge for your children that they are not alone in the world, you will begin to rebuild a sturdy foundation that is necessary for their emotional health.

One of the things children *can* do to help themselves and you is to help with the chores around the house. It's good medicine for them to pitch in to make life better again. By carrying the groceries, washing the dishes, or taking the dog for a walk, you give your child a chance to experience some amount of control over the world again. That doesn't mean you should throw the burden of running the household on them. Teamwork is the idea, group participation. Doing it *together* can make everyone feel better.

Their responsibilities should not include the psychological burden of any financial problems you may face. They will understand if the belt needs to be tightened, as long as you explain it. But you don't want them to lie awake at night worrying that you're all going to be thrown into the street. You have to decide where to draw the line. If you haven't experienced the role of disciplinarian, the person who says no, you'll have to learn. If you explain firmly and simply that everyone has to give up a little, most children will accept it.

My children are suffering more than they should. I don't feel I do them justice at times because I'm so wrapped up in my own feelings.

HELPING YOUR CHILD THROUGH GRIEF

There is no more terrifying experience for a child than losing a parent. You should prepare yourself for the storm that may overtake your usually happy and well-adjusted child. It's hard work and requires a great deal of patience, something you may not have in abundance right now. Your own energy may be very low, and your irritability level very high. Many widows feel guilt because they have enough to deal with themselves, and their children add to the pressure. You do the best you can.

Children, like adults, react to death in their own individual way. What may sound like an unreasonable response to you, "I hate you, and I hate Daddy," may be his way of releasing anger at a loss that is larger than life. The safety net that was Daddy is gone, and your child may actually feel in danger of complete abandonment. Some children exhibit intense anxiety, even panic. Others have trouble concentrating or become restless, aggressive, or hyperactive. Children sometimes have one cold after another, because stress and unexpressed feelings affect the immune system. They may be stoic and seem a little dazed or at times hysterical. Your child is hurting and needs your help.

I have two children, ages six and seven. I don't cry in front of them, and I think that someday they may feel that I didn't care. But still I feel that I have to protect them from grief and keep things as normal as possible for them. I hope one day we can sit down and talk and grieve together.

It's really a mistake to think that you have to be strong. Children need to express their sadness and anger and all the other emotions that go with the pain of loss. You don't allow that by saying, "You're a big girl now, and big girls don't cry," or by saying, "If your father could see you now, what would he think?" There's enough guilt in the world, and it shouldn't be loaded on the shoulders of a child.

How your child comes out of all this and reaches acceptance is largely up to you. There are no shortcuts through grief—not for widows and not for the children of widows. Everyone needs time and understanding and compassion.

FEAR

The death of a parent increases a child's fear of his or her own death and the death of the remaining parent. Life isn't dependable any-

173

more, and children really do worry about who will take care of them. This is an issue that *must* be dealt with. The very roots of their security have suddenly been taken away.

It's a good idea for everyone, including yourself, to have a medical checkup now so that everyone is reassured that they are healthy. Your health is of particular concern to your child. It should be explained that not all illnesses or accidents or emotional problems lead to death. If this discussion can be handled with your doctor or pediatrician present, it will make your child feel less vulnerable.

Assure your child that you expect to live for a long time, but you might want to go one step further. At some point after Martin died, I decided to arrange for legal guardianship for my children, just in case anything happened to me. I discussed it with them and chose a friend whose husband is a professional violinist. But my lawyer pointed out that most people assign guardianship assuming that the husband always predeceases his wife, and we all know that isn't necessarily true. The husband of the guardian I chose spent so much time away it would have been impossible for him to take care of my children—let alone his own—should his wife die first. When I realized my lawyer was right, that guardianship changed. If arranging for guardianship is something you feel better about doing, be sure to share it with your children.

Some younger children fear that if you leave the house, you'll never come back. Obviously, you can't allow their fear to hold you prisoner. Tell your child when you are leaving and when you will be back. Be on time. If you know you're going to be late, call and explain why and set the time for your return. Don't leave your child wondering and worrying. You might try leaving something personal of yours at home and in the care of your child so that he or she is sure that you'll be back.

My youngest is trying hard to accept and understand that the one person he loved most in the world is gone. He wants everything done now because he's afraid we'll all die soon and there isn't any time.

SLEEPING AND EATING PROBLEMS

Confusing emotions and fear can produce stress and anxiety in children. They may not be hungry for meals or may just pick at their food. Many children who otherwise sleep soundly may suddenly develop a fear of the night, the dark, and sleep. Explaining death as "being like sleep" or "an eternal sleep" can set it off. Some children think that if they fall asleep, they'll never wake up again. They can become sensitive to loud noises, like thunder or an ambulance screaming by the house. A child's fear of abandonment can cause nightmares, too. Many children experience these things as part of their normal development, but the death of a parent can increase the fear and cause the situation to be much more serious. Your own common-sense about what to do can guide you, but here are some specific suggestions:

- Soft blankets and even flannel sheets can be very comforting. You might try allowing your child to sleep without a top sheet, so that he or she is snuggled directly against a soft cover.

- Take a special moment to tuck your child in at night. A story before bedtime or a little good-night talk can be very reassuring.

- A night-light or a hall light that can be

dimly seen from your child's bedroom can make the darkness seem not quite so dark.

- The sounds of your presence in the house—a low playing radio or television —can act as a lullaby. The child knows you're there because he or she can hear you.

- If nightmares occur, you may have to be aware of your child's needs during the night. Your sleep time is important, too, but be patient and spend a few minutes helping your child settle down again.

My son spent his entire puberty in and out of the hospital waiting for his father to die. It was like the boy and I were part of some tableau, always standing in the hospital corridor waiting for the worst to happen.

Many widows find that they can't eat normal foods for a while, and some children react the same way. Most of us have memories of Mom serving up some special food during childhood illnesses, and those memories will serve you well now. The extra attention given when you prepare special foods for your child says you care. Everyone's diet should include nutritional foods and probably a vitamin supplement, but a little bit of indulgence is good for you and your child. Soft and creamy foods are easier to handle in the short run: applesauce, ice cream, a milk shake now and then. Warm foods that are easily digested will be the most appealing. For a while it may be best to stay away from spicy or fried foods or rough foods, like crackers and salty snacks. Emphasize soups and other foods that are soft, like mashed potatoes. Warm milk before bed can help a child relax and sleep. You probably don't have much of an appetite yourself and wouldn't appreciate anyone forcing you to eat. Be patient with your child's eating habits. It's important to be alert to keeping a balanced diet, but try to do it in a way that is understanding of how your child feels.

I feel it's time to take some action. My little girl has never cried. She's angry at home and especially at school. I worry about her.

EXPRESSING EMOTION

Not all children are comfortable openly showing their feelings. Some children prefer to cry when they're alone, perhaps when they're in bed and the lights are out and no one can see them. Or they may cry for some made-up reason rather than admit it's because they're sad about their father's death. But most children will follow your lead. If you are private, they will be private. If you shed tears and tell them that you're crying because you're sad, they'll understand that it's part of grief. I don't think there's anything more lonely than a solitary mourner, especially if he or she is a child. You're in this together as a family, and your individual and collective survival may depend on the way you handle the emotional needs of your children.

Don't cut them off when they need to communicate. If it's inconvenient—you're late for an appointment—all you can do is make sure that you follow up at a later time. Keep in mind that they have a need to share their thoughts and feelings. If you can, stop what you're doing, sit down with your child, and listen to what he or she has to say.

Some children, especially teenagers, may retreat from physical closeness, and I think you have to respect that. But you can try with any child by saying that you really could use a hug today. Tomorrow, he or she might ask you for one. With younger children, it's especially important that they receive warmth and closeness from you.

The family photo album can be a good way for all of you to grieve together. Remembering the wonderful moments with Dad can help the sadness to surface and the tears to flow.

I think it needs to be repeated: Don't hide your emotional feelings from your child. Tell them that you're sad, or angry—but not at them—because you miss Dad as much as they do.

As a teenager, my son asked for outside help. He said later that had he not gotten it, he would probably have committed suicide.

WHEN TO GET HELP

I had so much trouble dealing with my own feelings that I wasn't able to do enough for my children. I didn't seek professional help for myself or them soon enough, although we could have used it. Why? The answer is money. The knowledge that Martin had no life insurance panicked me, and I was too terrified to spend money on therapy or anything else. That is no excuse today. There are free programs available for children who have lost a parent. Check with your medical doctor, local church, or even the school to find counseling for your children if they need it. The messages they give through their behavior will tell you if it's necessary, or they may even ask for it. If you can't cope with their needs—and it's perfectly understandable if you can't—that should also tell you to seek assistance outside the family.

YOUR CHILDREN ARE WORTH IT

There were many days when I didn't think I would survive the problems I had with my children. Sometimes I wanted to run away. I hated them and the responsibility they represented. I loved them, too, but I can remember feeling that if one more thing went wrong, if one more crisis happened because of them, or me, or the rotten situation we were in, I would probably crack up.

Jon developed a terrible behavior problem

in school. His grades were abysmal. He was so difficult that he was asked to leave several schools—or 'asked not to come back,' as they put it more politely. He stifled his feelings (primarily rage) with marijuana and God knows what other drugs, or he would erupt like a volcano and terrorize his sister and me. I never knew where to find him, and for a number of years I feared that I would lose my son as well as my husband.

My daughter, Elizabeth, didn't rebel until her midteens, when she discovered nightclubs. That might have happened if her father had lived, but I doubt it. She is still working out her life, but I think she'd be having an easier time of it if she hadn't sustained that early trauma.

For all I went through with them, they turned out fine. That's the hope I can give you. When I look at my children today, I'm pleased. That's a good reason to do all you can for your children in what may be the most difficult time of their life. Once you've done that, with honesty, at some point it's up to them to move on, just as you must be able to move on.

8

REBUILDING
SELF-CONFIDENCE

Dear Lynn,

My husband died last spring after a long illness. We were married eighteen years, and our very deep love and happiness together made his death even more terrible for me.

The one thing I was not prepared for is the utter void I am in now. I work, have the blessings of good friends and the consolation of everyone. It's no good. It isn't enough to hold me together. I get these awful feelings of "Who am I?" Since I was nineteen years old, my husband had been my alter ego. Am I supposed to think of myself as the nineteen-year-old I was before I became a wife? He is all that's familiar and warm and "home" for me. I feel it's all gone, wiped out. I'm just half a person, or worse, there's no, "me" anymore. I'm thirty-seven years old, and I have no self-confidence. I feel inadequate making decisions and just completely stupid. I'm sure everyone knows I don't know what I'm doing. I have to arrange to sell various things in order to be able to live, but I'm afraid to talk to the lawyer. I don't know what to say or how to say it. My husband always took care of those things, never me. I'm afraid of the future and have a lot of self-doubt. Other people can handle things, why can't I?

It would be so easy if we had a formula to produce self-confidence. If it could be identified as something outside ourselves that we could obtain, all would be well. But self-confidence has an elusive quality. It's the kind of thing that has to do with trust and faith—like walking across a room and knowing that the floor is not going to collapse underneath you.

When you've experienced widowhood, you know that life can be unfair, even cruel, and that knowledge changes you. If someone you love can be taken from you—and it often feels that way—then anything can happen. What else can go wrong? You develop an understanding very quickly that life is fragile. You come to believe that the floor very likely could fall out from beneath you. And if the floor can go, then the walls and ceiling are probably not far behind.

Widowhood produces just such a domino effect. Your husband dies, your social status —and, in many cases, financial security—is at stake. The "we" that was part of your identity doesn't exist anymore. It may feel like someone else is calling the shots and that you are powerless. You may begin not to trust yourself, not to believe in yourself. You may be fearful and feel inadequate, without self-confidence, unable to deal with job interviews or the professional people you need to hire. The confidence in your ability to handle things; the self-esteem that you took for granted, maybe never even noticed, seems to be gone. How do you get a thing like that back?

The answer is you don't get it back. You rebuild it. You start over. The only way that rebuilding can happen is if you learn how to change *yourself*. The world will not alter to accommodate you, so you have to do the changing. You have to learn to change your way of dealing with people. You have to learn to change your attitude. You have to learn that you are not a victim. And, most important, you have to learn that the trust and faith you need comes from within *you*. There is no magic formula for self-confidence, and no one can give it to you. It's something you do for yourself.

I've been striving hard to get back to the person I was before my husband died. I can't though because I'm not the same person. Part of me died, too. Now I want to make the best of all that is left.

WHAT IS A WIDOW?

When I was promoting my book *Widow*, I appeared on a show in California and gave an interview that left a lasting impression on me. The interviewer asked me what came to mind when I thought of the word widow. I replied, as I wrote in *Widow*, that the word in Sanskrit means "empty," and I felt that was an appropriate description. He said no, that wasn't what he meant. "When I think of the word widow," he said, "I think of someone pitiful, dependent, a loser," and he continued with a number of other common put-downs. He said it to get a rise out of me, for the sake of the interview, and it did. I was so angry and thought, damn it, those words don't describe *me*. I said to him, "No, I will not accept that. I am not that way. I may feel a little frightened now, but I have a lot of qualities that I like about myself. I am not a loser. I have courage. I take risks. I am strong. I can make it. . . ." It was a terrific interview; very honest and intense. And while I was sitting there saying these things, all of a sudden my thinking started to change, and it opened up floodgates of self-confidence that had really been pushed down and buried. I didn't realize that I had simply accepted those labels for so long that I did identify myself with them. Many other widows do, too, and that's another thing you have to change.

I applied the same technique in my self-confidence classes, and I recommend that you try it, too. Sit down with a pad of paper, and write five words that describe widow or widowhood for you. Write them down and look at them and think about them. Is that really you? If you wrote inadequate, half a person, no person, dependent, or whatever, do you really think those words describe you? I'm here to tell you that it ain't necessarily so.

I feel like a lost soul. My confidence is shattered along with my physical being. How can I hope again, when I'm afraid. It's as though I'm back in school, only instead of failing math, I think I'm about to flunk the future.

IDENTIFYING YOUR STRENGTHS

If you lack self-confidence, you've probably already identified enough weaknesses to last you a lifetime. So I can give you another technique I used in my class. Get out your yellow pad and write down at least ten positive statements about yourself. When you're feeling weak and powerless, it's important to establish for yourself that you do have strengths. If you have trouble coming up with ten statements, ask your friends for help. You may not be completely aware of the image you project, and it can be valuable to know what they see. Don't make any negative statements at all. It's against the rules. The habit of harsh self-criticism is so strong in most of us that this exercise can be surprisingly tough to do.

In one class I gave, a widow got up to make her ten statements, and unlike the others in the group, described herself in glowing terms. What was this woman doing in my group, I wondered. She didn't need to be there. But she summed it up by saying, "And at the end of this course, I hope not only to say positive things about myself, but I hope to believe the positive things I say."

Once you start doing this, you'll become more aware of the difference between negative self-criticism and positive self-criticism, and you'll find that you aren't so quick to think the worst of yourself. When you get into the habit of seeing yourself in a much brighter light, you begin to think of yourself in a different way. By taking an inventory of your strengths and reminding yourself that you have them, you're patiently correcting and changing the old you. If you're feeling negative because you had a bad time today, take the list out and read it over. Or review it before the day begins or before you have to face a meeting or appointment. It's a matter of awareness and acceptance and understanding. It takes a little time, but it does get easier, and you will feel more and more positive about yourself as you go along.

Did I do the right thing living for him? I was his wife for most of my adult life. I feel like I've been fired from my job.

189

What am I supposed to do now? Who am I supposed to be now?

IDENTIFYING YOUR NEEDS

An effective method of blasting away at barriers to self-assurance is to establish what kind of confidence you want to build. When I first started doing this, at the top of my list was, "Don't be afraid." I didn't want to feel intimidated by everyone in the world, from relatives to professional people to my own children. Even my friends frightened me. They might tell me to go out and buy a low-cut dress when I wasn't ready for it, and I'd do it. I'd often do things that people told me to do because I felt intimidated. Maybe you want to run your life without interference from your family or handle your own finances. Or perhaps you want, or need, to find a job. If you list the types of confidence you want, it will give you a focus. It will make you aware of how you want to change.

At this point I am totally alone in the world and living in a strange new area as well. I'm still finding it difficult trying to make a "go of it" on my own. We seem to need approval time and time again,

190

until we discover it's only ourselves who need to be satisfied in the long run. I'm not sure I believe that yet.

EXTENDING CONFIDENCE

Martin was a lawyer. When he died and I no longer had him to rely on, I realized that I had difficulty dealing with the professional people I hired, even lawyers. Since then I don't know how many times I've heard that women—not just widows—are terrified of the people they hire: their lawyers, doctors, accountants. It's very important for all of us to understand that we are paying these people to do for us. They're not doing you a favor. When you're feeling weak or powerless, it's difficult to get past that. But it can be done.

You have to start out by hiring the right person. You usually find professional people through referrals from friends or other professionals. That's probably the best way. But remember that just because a person is good for your friend or relative, it doesn't necessarily mean that person is good for you. You should shop around to find the people who can do the best job for you. Particularly in early widowhood, when you may be so confused that you're really not sure what you need, it's very important to have preliminary consultations. And, damn it, if it doesn't feel right, trust yourself. If the old family retainer isn't for you, don't hire him. The hell with loyalty. You're alone now and have to think of yourself first. If you get that discomfort, if you feel someone is being unsympathetic or lacks understanding, that is not a person you want to pay your money to.

When you hire someone, you're paying for services to which you are entitled. If you're dealing with a professional and you don't understand something, you must be able to say, "I don't understand. Would you please explain that to me again." If you're uncomfortable with someone's solutions, you must be able to say, "That makes me uncomfortable. Is there another way we can do it?" And you've got to be able to go back later and follow up with additional questions or clarification. There's nothing wrong with calling or writing a letter after a meeting in order to be sure you know what you're agreeing to or what the consequences will be. Some of the decisions you're facing are the most important you will ever have to make, and they may have a far-reaching effect. You can't afford to be frightened, or feel stupid, or think that they won't like you. It's not a popularity contest.

No matter whom you're dealing with, or what you have to say or do, however difficult, there are a number of steps you can take to give yourself the best opportunity for a satisfactory outcome.

> He died without warning. He had a stroke. The dreadful loss of companionship, no longer someone watching out for us. It's a time of anguish, and I don't know how anyone can survive. I don't feel I'm capable.

DOING YOUR HOMEWORK

A widow I met in Tulsa told me a real horror story about what her lack of confidence and planning cost her.

She needed a lawyer to handle various business and real estate matters after her husband died and after the will was settled. She hired a lawyer. Two days later, she decided she had made a terrible mistake in hiring this lawyer, so she set about to find another one. She hired someone else, and a week later the same kind of doubt crept in. Now she was in a dilemma. She had two lawyers to whom she owed a retainer fee and didn't want to work with either of them. She found a third lawyer to get her out of the mess with the first two and, in the end, didn't want that lawyer either. Eventually, she settled on one lawyer, but obviously something was wrong with the way she approached the whole situation.

It's essential to prepare for preliminary meetings with professionals by making a list of what you want to talk to them about. You have got to be the one to know what you want because you, ultimately, have to make the final decision. If you realize after the preliminary meeting that you have additional questions, follow up. As I've said, there's nothing wrong with calling or sending a letter to clarify points. And if you don't want to make a commitment, it's perfectly OK to say, "Thank you for your time. I'll think about it."

As part of this yellow-pad planning session, it's a good idea to list what you want to know about the professional you may hire. Include questions like "What is your fee? Do you work on an hourly rate? When do I have to pay you? Have you handled things like this before?" Anyone who can't or won't answer your questions is probably not the right professional for you.

If the woman in Tulsa had done this, she probably would not have been so quick to sign a retainer agreement with anyone. Instead, she would have had the meeting, gone home, and reviewed her list of questions and the answers she received. She would have given some thought to whether or not she was comfortable with this person. And based on all the things she learned, she would have been better equipped to make a decision.

REHEARSING

Once you have an idea of what you want from the professional you need to hire or you've set up a job interview, or meeting, the next step is to practice communicating effectively. I was literally *driven* to look into communication skills because so many times I went home from a meeting and hated myself because I had been wishy-washy. I never seemed to get what I wanted. I felt put down, foolish, inadequate.

I have a friend in Los Angeles, a widow who went back to work soon after her husband died. She had to hire a live-in housekeeper because she had a young son at home.

The first one didn't work out very well, and the time came when it was obvious that the housekeeper would have to go. But my friend couldn't face the woman and fire her. She was a competent, highly paid advertising executive and had never reacted this way before. At the time I couldn't understand how she could have such a problem. At the time I still had a husband.

Weeks went by while she gave herself pep talks and mental confidence boosters, and finally she told the woman to leave. She told me later that she had spent those weeks periodically rehearsing exactly what she would say. She practiced it mentally and verbally, and when the evening came to lower the boom on her employee she was able to do it.

When you're learning or relearning any skill, you have to rehearse. Practice, practice, practice—I won't say it makes you perfect, but it sure makes you better!

Each day I find myself believing that there is a "me" inside this body—not just what's left of a twenty-year partnership.

IMPROVING COMMUNICATION

There are two valuable tools you can use

when you start to work on your communication skills: a mirror and a tape recorder. The mirror will be of particular help when you're working on nonverbal communication; that is what you say with your body movements, such as your hands or your facial expressions. Some people refer to it as "body language." It's just as important as the words you use and the way your voice sounds because it carries messages to the person you're speaking to. Using a mirror and tape recorder may feel a little awkward at first, but, believe me, the results of your efforts will please you.

- Start by standing in front of the mirror. Pretend that you're addressing the person you will be meeting. Pay attention to your body posture. Relax your shoulders and keep your head erect. The mirror will help to refine the nonverbal messages you send to others.

- You would begin any meeting with eye contact, by looking at the other person in a relaxed and steady manner. You don't want to be like the little victim with the downcast eyes.

197

- Notice where your hands are. Fidgeting is a dead giveaway. You shouldn't play with your hands or shuffle your feet around. Stay comfortably still and sit or stand straight. Don't toy with a button or a strand of hair or a piece of jewelry.

- Your facial expressions should be consistent with the rest of your body message, which is determined, yet relaxed. If you look like a pitiful creature, that is the message you will convey. If you look relaxed and determined, that is the message you will convey. There's no question which one is more likely to get you what you want.

- Sometimes when you're frightened your voice trembles. It takes a little practice to control a nervous tremor, and this is the time to do a breathing exercise. Simply take a slow deep breath and hold it for a count of three. Exhale slowly. Try it a couple of times, and you'll notice your voice will begin to steady.

- Work with a tape recorder so you can

be aware of the quality of your voice. Most of us really don't know how we sound. Speak slowly and clearly. Pause when it's appropriate. You don't have to keep up a continuous stream of chatter and compulsive talking. If you've thought out what you're going to say and you've made a list of points you want to make, this shouldn't be a problem.

- You can use a little physical activity as a way of loosening up and preparing for a meeting before you leave home. Try jumping up and down for a few minutes to get the circulation going. Or swing your arms—up to the sky and down to the ground—or move from side to side, wrapping your arms around you. Moving around like this often calmed me a little when I had to speak to someone I was nervous about. It helps to take away some of the tension.

THE REAL THING

You may be thinking, "It's a snap to do all of this in the privacy of your own home, but to take it out of the house and into a lawyer's office is quite another story." Sure it's a tall order, but you don't have much choice. Don't let fear work on you. You can build confidence by practicing out in the real world, too. Each time you go to another appointment or you have to deal with another situation, it gets easier. It becomes more familiar. Once you accept the fact that no one is going to bite you, you won't be so afraid.

I realized I've always identified myself as "we." It's time I became a more complete, self-sufficient person. I have hope, but it will take time. I have my ups and downs, but I can do it.

ATTITUDE

I've known many people who seem to handle difficult situations fearlessly, but who truthfully don't always know what they're doing. I mean that they're no more an expert at it than you or I. I'd always be amazed when friends would get what they wanted. I think I found one of the reasons—they fake self-confidence. I used to remind myself of that before leaving the house on the days when I felt particularly insecure. I used a little singsong phrase that I'd silently repeat to myself, "If you can't make it, fake it," or Mohammad Ali's line "I'm the greatest." I'd pretend that I was full of self-confidence and that nothing could phase me. It usually worked quite well, but there were still days when I came home dragging my chin on the floor. Some little thing a person said or did could set me off and it would bring me back to how fragile I still was. Widowed or not, I think we all know what it's like to feel as though you're taking one step forward and two steps back. So you deal with it one day at a time, and if that's too much, you take it by the hour. Approaching the world with all the self-confidence tools you can muster doesn't absolutely guarantee success. That's when you have to know that it isn't necessary for you to be perfect. Just because you may have failed to achieve an objective one day, doesn't mean it's Last Chance Café and that you can't start again tomorrow. Of course you can. You have to get out there and try the next day, and the next, and the next.

There's nothing in the world like learning how to repair a toilet, or cementing in a mailbox pole, or replacing the lock on the front door. I can't afford to have repair

201

people in for every little thing, so I took my husband's toolbox and started doing things myself. Some of my work looks pretty bad, but nothing has exploded or fallen over yet. It feels good to take care of things on my own.

PUTTING IT TO WORK

One of the ways you demonstrate self-confidence is by doing. It's not necessary to achieve a knock-your-socks-off success, although that's wonderful if it happens. When you take action, however unimportant it may seem, you make a statement about yourself. And you should listen to it. You're saying what I said that day at the television show. "I may feel a little frightened now, but I have a lot of qualities that I like about myself. I have courage. I take risks. I am strong. I can make it." The fact is, I walked out of the studio after the interview feeling exhilarated because I realized I had more faith in myself than I thought I had. That day I took a small step toward trusting myself again, toward acknowledging that there is indeed an "I," a Lynn Caine, a whole person. That's self-confidence!

9

THE ASSERTIVE WIDOW

Dear Lynn,

I know the shock and numbness and the grief. I went through it all—the anger, the sorrow, the men, the loneliness, and I am sick of well-meaning people telling me it will get better or that they know how I feel. How the hell does anyone know how I feel? You have to be there to understand. No one else can.

We don't belong to a church, and if one more person tells me it was God's will or there must be a plan, I am going to hit that person in the face! I am tired of people telling me I am brave and courageous. Even my two sons (thirteen and fifteen) have better sense than that. Maybe I'm being dramatic, but I've been a widow for sixteen months, and I have had enough. I remember telling someone there should be a list for widows of gracious answers when some loose-brained idiot asks you in the funeral parlor such questions as "You are broke aren't you?" or "I 'spect you'll be getting remarried soon." Who the hell do these people think they are?

I know most people mean well, but it makes me so angry when friends think they know what's best for me or for my children. Everyone is an expert when it comes to what I should be doing. I get impatient and even had an argument with my sister when I told her to mind her own business. I get very upset with people who have words of wisdom for me all the time.

People often feel uncomfortable talking to widows and to the bereaved in general. They're so afraid of saying the wrong thing that they usually *do* say the wrong thing. Even though we have come a long way in our willingness to understand death and dying and a lot of research goes on, people still don't find it all that easy to deal with. I know many adults who are able to talk about the meaning of death, about "the other side," the possibility of reincarnation, the near-death experience, and all kinds of other issues surrounding death. But when someone's husband dies, a lot of people become uncomfortable and don't know what to say.

I think one of the most well-meaning, but ultimately insulting things one can say to a bereaved person is, I know how you feel, when most people couldn't possibly know how I feel.

When people don't know what to say, they're capable of saying all kinds of inappropriate things. Some remarks are seemingly unkind—"It must be really lousy to be a widow" (someone actually said that to a friend of mine)—and others are unknowingly cruel—"You better find somebody soon, 'cause you're not going to last long without a man."

Widows are constantly confronted with insensitive questions and unsolicited advice. Everyone wants to give it, whether you want it or not. How do you reply when family and friends tell you that you should get married again, move out of your home, or take a trip or question you about when you're going to start dating or how much money your husband left you?

While psychologists and sociologists may

be familiar with the impact of death, the layman finds himself unprepared and the culture around him antagonistic to his reactions. No one wants to tolerate an angry, grief-filled person dealing with the death of a loved one.

It isn't much help to realize that inappropriate remarks are usually made because of ignorance, not malice. Even mental-health professionals are not immune to blurting out some foolish, even impertinent, comment, when they're feeling awkward about facing a grieving person.

Shortly after my husband's death, a psychiatrist in my building crossed the street when he saw me. Enraged, I crossed after him, looked him in the eye, and inquired about his family, just as I would have at any other time. After all, he was my neighbor. Our children played together. Avoiding my eyes, he blurted out, "Oh, Lynn, how are . . . how is everything in your miserable life?"

That is only one of the many hurtful comments made to me after I became widowed. Frequently, I was at a loss for words. Like most widows, I was afraid to express anger, afraid it was unladylike. I was also afraid that if I did show anger, no one would like me anymore. Only later would I think of the response I wish I'd made. How many times I'd ask myself, "Why didn't you say *that* instead of just standing there like a dummy?"

If you've experienced this, you know it is quite a shock to have a person drop a bombshell like "What are you going to do about your sex life?" when there is no way, under any *other* circumstances, a stranger, friend, or family member would ever ask such a question. Most of us are familiar with the inability to respond, and the woman who wrote about the need for a list of gracious answers won't find any disagreement from me.

My friend Laura kept a record of what people said to her after her husband died. The comments and questions are so startingly similar, that Laura said, "I was astonished by the lack of originality. Uppermost in everyone's mind seemed to be that I should get married again. They told me with surprise in their voices that I was strong and that I looked terrific, as if widowhood should have produced some radical alteration in my appearance. They advised me to move, start dating as soon as possible, and not to talk about my husband to men!"

207

A survey was taken a few years ago in which a group of bereaved people was interviewed to find out their reactions to comments others make. The result was that the majority of remarks generally heard were considered unhelpful. These were mainly expressions of advice or an interpretation of the widow's situation: "Snap out of it and stop feeling sorry for yourself"; "You've got to get out more and meet people." The other kind was the comment that ignores the feelings of the bereaved person: "Death comes to us all"; "You'll find someone to love again."

The smallest percentage of questions or comments were those that were considered helpful: "What can I do to help?" "Can I recommend a lawyer, or is there some other professional advice you need?" These kinds of comments acknowledge that a person has feelings and are respectful of grief.

It seems to me that we could all use a little education in this area.

Like me, Laura would stifle her feelings and become deeply depressed, or she'd have a delayed reaction and boil over with rage. So there is a double whammy. People make insensitive remarks, and widows respond by lashing out or becoming speechless. At least that's the way most widows react. Both reactions are inappropriate, destroy self-esteem, and can be handled much better with a few simple techniques of assertiveness training.

If I hear once more how good I look or how brave I am, I will scream.

UNDERSTANDING BEHAVIOR PATTERNS

I've taught many assertiveness-training courses over the years and know that the first step in learning about what you *can* be is recognizing what you already are. By that I mean that understanding your own behavior patterns—and everyone has them—can be an enormous help in reshaping the way you act, the way you respond to others, and the way you handle yourself. So I start off my training classes by defining three major behavior categories and letting participants see which pattern they fit into. See if you recognize yourself.

NONASSERTIVE, PASSIVE BEHAVIOR

The majority of widows fit into this category

or some variation of it. The nonassertive widow doesn't respect her own rights, though she may respect the rights of others. She allows people to say unkind or hurtful things to her, and she doesn't know how to reply, or just can't seem to open her mouth to say anything at all. She is fearful of expressing her feelings, if, indeed, she is in touch with them.

She often says yes when she means no. She is the ultimate people pleaser. She fears that she cannot exist without the approval of others. She doesn't act, she reacts. The nonassertive widow allows others to tell her what to do. She is indecisive and often depressed. (The classic definition is "anger turned against yourself.") She feels helpless and hopeless, and all too often her lack of self-respect provokes contempt and rejection in spite of all her efforts to please.

AGGRESSIVE BEHAVIOR

This is often confused with assertive behavior, but the two couldn't be more different. The aggressive widow is belligerent, abusive, judgmental. Often a widow will announce in one of my groups, "Lynn, you'll be so proud of me. I really told off my neighbor." Telling someone off is not assertive, it's aggressive. The aggressive widow is not the one who considers telling people what to do with their advice, she does tell them, loud and clear. She hurts, humiliates, and manipulates. She feels lonely, unwanted, depressed, and, believe it or not, insecure.

ASSERTIVE BEHAVIOR

This is worth working for. The assertive widow respects both her own rights and the rights of others. She is straightforward and honest. She expresses her feelings directly and accepts responsibility for them. Consequently, she is usually successful in fulfilling her needs and in getting her feelings across to others. She has a better chance of maintaining old relationships and at the same time attracting new ones.

Sounds good, doesn't it?

It takes some attention, but it's not as difficult as you may think.

Soon after my husband's death, I went to buy a gravestone. It was very painful for me. The lady in charge of the place greeted me cheerily with "Mrs. Puck, you are a lucky lady today. During this entire month, we're giving away green stamps with every purchase."

LEARNING TO BE ASSERTIVE— THE TECHNIQUES

FEEL THE HOOKS

Every time I was the target of an insensitive remark, I felt as if a hook had been thrown into me. Terrified of confrontation, my ability to speak reasonably withered away. Usually I'd say nothing and stuff the painful feelings down inside in a typically nonassertive way. Or I'd explode in an aggressive rage because I could no longer contain my stifled feelings. Finally, when I permitted myself to feel and acknowledge the hooks, I noticed that a little red light went on in my head. When that happened, I could recognize my feelings and know when I needed to be assertive. It just made me stop and think about it, and then I learned to act accordingly.

You know what infuriates me most of all? It's when the visit-the-bereaved-widow types visit (uninvited) and say with their

212

sanctimoniously saccharine smiles, "Oh, you're so brave, you're just an inspiration to us all." Who in the hell had any damn alternative?

SEND THE "I" MESSAGE

Of all the techniques recommended in assertiveness-training manuals and of all those I've used in my classes, the "I" message has proved to be the easiest and the most effective. Once I felt the hook and the red light went on, I acknowledged my feelings—anger, discomfort, defeat, whatever—and I was able to express them simply and directly as long as I began my sentence with "I." Here are some examples:

"I feel uncomfortable with that suggestion."

"I am not ready to go out on dates."

"I prefer to stay home next weekend."

"I need some time to make that decision."

Sentences beginning with the word "you" tend to be accusatory, judgmental, aggressive, and not assertive.

"You have no right to ask me when I intend to start dating."

"You make me feel that something is wrong with me."

By using the "I" message, you are being honest. When you look someone in the eye and express your feelings, your beliefs, and your needs in a calm and straightforward way, you are able to deal directly with criticism or advice. It's such a simple technique that you'll wonder why you haven't used it all your life, in every potential confrontation.

I was surprised to find out how bitter I was toward people who sincerely wanted to help, but were unable to because of their own fear of death. They couldn't face me. I think they were afraid of how they'd act. One neighbor who used to be a Saturday afternoon chat-over-the-back-fence kind of friend has avoided me ever since my husband died six months ago.

214

ASK FOR CLARIFICATION

Some questions and comments require clarification before you can choose your reply, and it is your right to ask for it. Frequently, when you ask for clarification, the person who is offering advice or questioning you has a chance to reconsider what they've said. Remember that most people don't mean to offend you. They feel uncomfortable dealing with your loss and say things out of ignorance or embarrassment.

> A man psychiatrist friend of ours advised me at five months to be looking around for another man. He said my children needed a father. Who would have wanted me, so engrossed in grief as I was and am? And didn't he think I had noticed that my children were fatherless and that they were in pain about it?

When I was faced with a thoughtless comment like that, and I was, I often found it helpful to say, "I don't understand what you mean. Would you please repeat what you said"; or "Do I understand you to mean . . ."; or "I want to understand you correctly." A request for clarification is assertive, not aggressive.

PLAY THE BROKEN RECORD

After you've used the "I" message calmly and quietly or you've requested clarification and someone still persists—"Just how long do you intend to stay in that big house all by yourself?"—you can try this method.

If your original reply was "I am not ready to make that decision yet," just keep repeating that response. Do it quietly and calmly. Don't get rattled or caught up in a discussion and overtalk your point. Just repeat it. "As I told you, I'm not ready to make that decision yet." From my own experience, I know that eventually they *will* get the message.

Everyone assures me that time heals all, which is undoubtedly true. However, one doesn't live with a person for thirty-four years and overcome the loneliness and heartbreak very soon, if ever. It makes me wonder how people can say such things without really knowing what the loss is all about.

USE FOGGING

This technique was developed by Manuel J. Smith, author of *When I Say No I Feel Guilty* (Bantam Books, 1985), to cope with manipulative criticism. It teaches us to agree with any truth in the statements people use to criticize us. Look for whatever truth is present (however small) in the comment, pull it out, and make it part of your response.

"If you didn't compare every man you dated with Martin, you'd be married by now."

The fogging response: "You're right." You could also say, "That's probably true" or, "I agree. If I didn't make comparisons, I'd probably be married again. When I no longer feel the need to compare, I'll stop doing it." Another response is "I can certainly understand why you think that."

How can your well-meaning, but critical, friend or relative disagree with that? By taking a statement and finding the truth and using it, you can defuse a thoughtless remark.

My husband was an editor, and two weeks after he died, one of his authors—a famous author—came up to me and looked at me with a straight frown and squinty eyes as if I'd stolen his wallet and said: "How could you? He was my editor. How could you let him die?" And he really meant that. I couldn't believe it. It was as if to say, "He was only your husband, but for God's sakes, he was my editor. I can't write without him." And the fact was that he couldn't. He never again wrote an important book.

When someone suggests, "It's time to pull yourself together. He's been dead over a year," try replying, "I realize there is a myth that a widow should be done with mourning in one year. In truth, there is no timetable, and, according to the literature, it's a rare widow who is over it in a year."

Here you are using the "I" message and being authoritative. Nothing used to enrage me as much as this statement. "How in the hell do you know?" I always felt like saying. "Let's see how you feel when your time comes." I never answered that aggressively, but I used to think it a lot. The "I" message and a simple statement of fact is far more effective, and there is less likelihood of losing a friend.

How about all the people who tell you that you should get away? "Go take a trip." It's hard enough to eat dinner alone, much less to travel. Furthermore, chances are you need the comfort of familiar objects. And no matter what anyone says, you should not get rid of your husband's things until you feel ready to do so.

Here's an opportunity to use fogging.

"Yes, I agree that travel is marvelous, but I'm not ready to take any trips."

If they persist, "But it will do you good to get away," use the broken record. "I am not ready to travel." "I am not ready to travel." "I'm not ready to travel." Stay with it and stay calm.

"When are you going to take off your wedding ring?"

My first thought: "It's none of your damned business." But since it's better to be assertive than aggressive, try saying, "I don't really know when I'll be ready. I'm not right now."

BEING ASSERTIVE

Armed with these basic techniques, you will be able to deal with even the most prying questions and outrageous remarks. You are ready to be an assertive widow. Now let's see how it works.

"Did he leave you enough money to live on?"

No one dared to question you about your husband's income when he was alive, yet many people feel free to do so when he's dead. Financial information is for you to volunteer if you wish to do so. Most widows—even those with secure finances—are terrified about lack of money. If someone is sincerely concerned about your financial situation, the way to show it is by presenting you with a sealed envelope containing cash or a check. You may feel like saying so, but that would be aggressive. Instead try:

"I really feel uncomfortable about discussing finances right now." That's honest, and you're using the "I" message.

"I leave my finances in my lawyer's hands."

Or you can use humor. I consider it the highest level of skill.

"I'd love to tell you, but I'm sworn to secrecy."

Yet the well-meaners are always saying, "Will you let me know if you need anything?" You expect anyone who is around and in touch to know that you need company, sympathetic listeners, a friend to help with errands, chores, and meals. If you have children, a baby-sitter is always welcome. I was once tempted to quote Dorothy Parker, when she said: "Get me a new husband."

> The friends we had all spurned me. They all have cars (I can't drive), but not one of them ever followed through on an offer to give me a lift to go shopping even in the bitter winter months. Somehow I think God is watching them and taking them into account.

Try to remember that most people really do want to help, but don't know how to express it. It takes generosity to accept the generosity of others. Accept the offer if you need help with something. Undoubtedly, there will be an opportunity for you to reciprocate. Be specific when you say yes:

"Thank you. Would you please pick up my dry cleaning tomorrow morning?"

"It would be enormously helpful if you'd take my cat to the vet on Thursday at one o'clock."

"I can't face the supermarket. Would you please shop for me tomorrow?"

You get the idea. If you take someone up on their offer, you'll soon find out who sincerely wants to help.

THE NEED TO
EXPRESS YOURSELF

An assertive widow can stand up to criticism or just plain dumb questions and comments in a positive way. I think it's worth repeating that most people would be surprised to learn that they have hurt your feelings or added to your grief by saying something out of turn. But it really isn't your problem to educate others, so don't worry about it. Worry about how *you* feel.

I always feel better when I remain calm and answer a question directly and honestly.

I don't get angry because of another person's stupidity or ignorance, and I don't suffer guilt from throwing an insulting remark back in someone's face. I just don't do that. I think widows have enough problems with anger and guilt without creating more through aggressive behavior.

Assertiveness is a way to fulfill the need to express your own opinion and feelings, but not by adding fuel to the fire. It is a constructive method of communication and might help save a friendship or family relationship at a time when you really need it.

10

CREATING A NEW SOCIAL LIFE

Dear Lynn,

After my husband died of cancer, I had to face widowhood and its overwhelming adjustments at the age of forty-two. Our former friends provided little in the way of help or consolation. They paid condolence calls, of course, but after that they practically disappeared. I hardly hear from any of them anymore, and I guess they're involved in their own problems. I don't feel I have anyone to talk to or one real friend. My children are grown-up, but they have their own lives to lead. I don't want to depend on them, and I'm sure they don't want me to. I hate being lonely. Sometimes I fear my own life more than I did his death.

I did receive some vague invitations from friends: "Oh you must come for the weekend sometime soon" or "Let's get together for dinner." They never follow up. I'm sure they have no intention of having a single woman around their husbands. Then there are the neighbors who simply don't invite you over on the weekend because there's no man for their husbands to talk to. It amazes me that people I've known for fifteen years and more would treat me like that, but they do. You'd think I was a total stranger. It hurts me, and I can tell you this, my dear husband would be furious if he knew how his so-called friends treated his widow. But what do I do, I want friends of my own. I just don't know how to start. I feel foolish. How am I supposed to make friends?

When you feel the need to be around people again, when you want friendship and companionship again, then it's time to go out into the world and make it happen. If you're lucky enough to receive invitations from old friends, by all means accept them. Even if you're not meeting new people but just visiting those you already know, you can consider the experience a rehearsal. Just being around people in a social situation will help you to get things going. It may not be easy, but it's helpful. I didn't receive many invitations from old friends, and especially lacking were invitations from couples that were friends before Martin's death. I've found that most widows experience the same thing.

Couples that were friends before you became a widow tend to fall to the wayside, particularly if they were primarily your husband's friends. Before Martin died, a key relationship for me was with his best friend and wife. We shared dinners, vacations, and weekends together and always made a good foursome. They were a major part of our social life. After Martin died and the foursome became a threesome, the friendship didn't work anymore. I felt like a friend-in-law and quickly realized that I couldn't rely on them for my social or emotional needs.

For the first few months or so you just get through what has happened, but after a while things begin to slow down, friends don't drop by or call as often, and you are left to fend for yourself. I don't feel I have much in common with them anymore.

Your changing relationship with couples is one of the most dramatic indications that your life is different, that you have to start over again. I felt anger and hurt and total betrayal when that friendship didn't continue as it had. In retrospect, it's clear that everyone got carried away with the drama of the situation and we all overextended ourselves. They took charge of my life, and I let them. They resented me. I resented them for resenting me, and our friendship deteriorated very quickly.

Years have passed since then, and we are now part of each other's lives again. Our relationship didn't go back to the way it was. It couldn't without Martin. But maybe it's better, stronger for what we have been through together. It took time for forgiveness and distance between us to gain perspective on a friendship I once again value very highly.

There are glorious exceptions to this. Older widows are usually more accepted by their couple friends. Every case is different. But in general, I think you have to make new friends, and the sooner the better.

I am mentally young, spirited, and used to be very active. I've always liked being around people, but I don't know where to turn to start over. I realize that I have always been a "we" and it's time I became a more complete person.

For many of us, going back into a social world alone isn't all that easy. It may be a long time since you had to take a bold step in getting to know new people. You need friendship, companionship, someone to talk to and to share experiences with. We all need that in our lives. There are things you can do that will help. One step may lead you to a new friend—male or female—but you must take the first step for anything at all to happen.

Two years after my husband's death I can look back and say, "You've come a long way baby!" and feel good about myself. I have a part-time job in a gift shop and do volunteer work at a local rehabilitation center. I'm meeting lots of new people, and I'm very happy being able to help others.

LIKE ATTRACTS LIKE

It's important that you follow your interests and develop new ones. If you're doing something you like, that turns you on, you have energy, enthusiasm, and vitality, and that in itself makes you attractive to other people.

Take some time to sit down and make a list of the things you do well or the things you've always wanted to do. Perhaps you have an interest in real estate, or the stock market, or gardening, or a foreign language. It's best to begin to build your new social life from an interest because there is such a thing as the power of attraction. You want to be with like-minded people. Following your interests will put you in an environment where you can meet them. Create your new social life on a firm foundation among people who like to do the same things you do.

An appreciation of music was a social pleasure Martin and I shared all through our marriage. After Martin died, I couldn't bear to hear music of any kind. It was just too painful. After a while, I finally decided that it was bad enough to be deprived of my husband, but that I didn't want to go through the rest of my life without music. I agree with Friedrich Nietzsche, who said, "Life without music is a mistake." So I forced myself to go alone to a performance of *The Marriage of Figaro*. Even though it's a comic opera, I quietly sobbed throughout aria after

229

aria as memories of Martin welled up inside me. I was in agony. I knew I'd made a mistake in forcing myself to sit through such torture, but I was too embarrassed to get up and leave. A woman sitting to my right was watching me with concern, and during the intermission she lightly touched my hand and asked if she could be of help. I felt like a blubbering idiot, but she was very kind and so I told her what was wrong. We talked until the curtain went up again, and I was able to sit and listen to the rest of the performance. We never met again, but I've never forgotten that night. The experience made it easier for me to listen to opera from then on. She was a stranger, and yet she was full of compassion. She didn't become a close friend, but she might have. It made me realize how important it is not to cut yourself off from things you enjoy doing and to take on new interests. They can serve as your lifeline back to the human race.

By starting out alone, I think I did it the hard way. If I had joined an opera group, it might not have been so tough. With just a little bit of planning, you can make it easier on yourself. Once you have a list of interests, look around for a way to follow through on one or more of them. Most towns and cities have some form of adult education available. Your local church, college, or museum may sponsor activities. If money is not an issue in your life, there are plenty of organizations that need volunteers. Make phone calls, talk to people. You have to make the effort to get things going again, and you'll find that one thing leads to another.

I now realize how much women need women friends. Being a sharer and a decent listener, I've found my honest friends feel quite alone much of the time, even if they're not widows. We'd all do well to cultivate our strengths rather than waiting for a man to fulfill all our needs. My women friends are a source of strength for me.

KNOWING THAT YOU CAN DO IT

Your greatest asset is a positive attitude. Meeting new people may be a bit frightening, but it's important that you enter your new social life with enthusiasm. All you need to start is one friend. You're not trying to fill Yankee Stadium. Be easy on yourself, and remember that it may take a little time. I know a widow who kept a note to herself on a bathroom mirror about the choices she faced each day:

I have chosen to do something to better my circumstances, and I will do it today.

Her choices are the same as yours: to approach life with enthusiasm or to approach it with a sense of defeat. She was socially active, and I think a lot of it had to do with looking at the world in a positive way. She wasn't a Pollyanna who walked around with a false smile on her face all the time, but a woman who believed, who really knew, that her life would be good again. You have to psych yourself up and get yourself going if you want to meet new people. Keep in mind that you do have choices: You can have a positive attitude or a negative attitude. If you choose the latter, you'll find out soon enough that a negative attitude turns people off, and you need people in your life. Try putting a little note to yourself on a mirror or the refrigerator as a reminder. A couple of reminders I've used are:

Take the first step, and the rest will follow.

I have the power to choose what my attitude will be toward this day's offerings. My attitude will make this day what it becomes.

There is nothing but NOW. We cut ourselves off from life by dwelling on what was, or what may be.

I saw a poster of a butterfly sometime ago. It said, "You can fly, but that cocoon has to go." I wrote it down on a piece of paper and keep it on my desk. It reminds me, when I need it, not to let my fears keep me from living again.

YOU GO FIRST

Don't sit back and *wait* for people to invite you places. Take the initiative and open your mouth, pick up the phone, make the effort to start things rolling. If everyone just sat around waiting for someone else to extend an invitation, no one would go anywhere! Creating a new social life includes men and women, and in either case you might wind up being the one who has to take the first step. I've never been very comfortable asking a man out, but I've done it a couple of times. Many of the younger women I know feel it's fine, while the older ones tend to feel awkward about it. I think you have to understand your own level of comfort when asking a man out and also take into consideration what you know about how the man will respond. If he says yes, I guess you can figure you've done the right thing.

Your social life includes women, too. Sadly, it seems some women would rather spend an evening with an inadequate male than with a female who is interesting and capable of being fun. It's really too bad. An attitude like that automatically cuts off a lot of possible friendships.

A widow I know who has been through a few relationships with men always says, "The men come and go, but my women friends are constant. They're the ones who see me through the tough times. I value those friendships and take care of them." I agree completely with that. But for all our awareness about women's rights, needs, and liberation, why is it still true that when some women say they're alone, that they have no one, what they really mean is, "I don't have a man." The woman who consoled me at the opera reminded me of how important my friendships with women have been.

After three years I find that one does survive and rebuild, but how much easier it would have been just to talk with another person, a friend who would be a listener about the despair and frustration. It's getting easier now, and I know if I keep trying things will get better.

PLAYACTING

Wishing won't make it so, but acting "as if" will. Acting as if you feel positive when you feel negative enables you to control the way you feel and act. The behavior you imitate becomes real.

For a long time, I didn't believe that I could lead a fulfilling, emotionally satisfying life without Martin. I was certain I was doomed to a fear-filled, lonely future. I was self-pitying, resentful, and did I collect injustice!

"Nobody wants you when you're a widow."

"Where are my friends and family now that I need them?"

"Don't they know how rotten I feel?"

I took inventory constantly and kept tabs on my mental scoreboard:

Who called?

How often?

Who extended invitations?

Who didn't?

Finally, I realized that I was beginning to turn off my friends and colleagues at a time I most needed a support system. Few people want you when you're needy. That's a law of human nature, just like no one invites you to a dinner party when you're hungry.

The laws of nature don't change, so you have to change if you want your gloom to lift. When I could stand my misery no longer, I discovered the magic of acting "as if."

Even though I didn't feel like it, I reached out and expressed interest in other people.

To my surprise, they expressed interest in me.

I forced myself to smile—at bus drivers, salespeople, my nasty landlord. To my surprise, they all smiled back.

I acted as if I didn't resent friends who had stopped calling, and I called them. To my surprise, they began calling me again.

I acted as if I felt energetic when I felt logy. To my surprise, my lethargy disappeared as soon as I got out and became active.

Finally, I acted as if I had the courage to confront the situations that frightened me. I began to take action—baby step by baby step—and I found that fear defies the law of perspective because the closer you get to the feared object, the smaller it becomes.

I don't claim that I changed overnight. It was a long battle with many setbacks. Still is. And it requires continuous action.

The world is not necessarily angry or hostile, but it can be fearful. Acting "as if" dispels fear and enables you to connect with others so you can begin either a new relationship or build on one that already exists.

I have been widowed for three years and still find it very difficult to have a social

237

life. I feel awkward eating in restaurants alone, so I hardly ever go out. Also, while I love to travel, I just cannot face the idea of going on tour alone, even though I know I will meet people on the way.

SEEING IT

I remember watching a special report on the Olympics a few years ago that explored some of the newer training techniques used to make champions out of athletes. The idea seems very simple. You picture in your mind what you want to have happen. Hold the picture for a moment, making sure that every detail is right. Then let go of it, meaning dissolve the picture from your mind and your thoughts. Athletes do this over and over again until the conditions, their coordination, their concentration, the execution of the feat, and the final result are *exactly* the way they want them to be. I don't know if anyone knows why, but it seems to work. I figure if it's good enough for Mary Lou Retton, it's good enough for me.

To use it in creating your own social life, just picture yourself in a social scene interacting with people. This visualizing is a kind of freewheeling daydreaming exercise, and you control what the dream is. Keep the picture fairly simple. See yourself in the day-dream, and visualize yourself having a good time with people, talking and laughing and making new friends. Then let the pictures of your daydream fade away, dissolve them, and see what happens. I can't recommend this as a miracle solution, but try it a few times, and perhaps you'll have some interesting results.

No friends rallied around me. I came home alone the day after the funeral. I cleaned out his closet and sat with all his stuff in the kitchen for a long time. A few weeks later, I called a local widows' group, but they told me they only dealt with older widows. I called another organization and went to one of their discussion evenings, although I had to force myself. I met Alice and Cathy that night. They've been wonderful to me, and their friend-ship means everything. I'd even go so far as to say that they have helped me to find the courage to go on.

11

DATING AND SEXUALITY

Dear Lynn,

It was Sunday afternoon when my husband died. He went to pick up my mother for dinner (she lives near us) and never made it. A drunk driver hit him broadside, and my husband was killed instantly.

I can say from experience that being a widow is the pits no matter how it happens. I've been alone for almost a year now, and I have a terrible need for comfort, the physical and emotional comfort and support a dearly beloved husband gives to a wife. I'm lonely and I feel like a misfit.

It seems as if our world is couple oriented, and if you're not part of a couple, you're made to feel either like some kind of freak or a person to be pitied. I feel depressed, like I'm being excluded from life. I find it hard to see my future. It frightens me to think about it. I don't want to be alone, but I'm afraid that is my future. It sounds like a bad joke, but there are things I want to do in bed other than read.

I miss so many things. Our long talks were wonderful. It seems we never ran out of things to say, I guess because we traveled a lot. How could I ever hope to have that in my life again?

My husband left me well provided for, so money is not a real issue. I can't go out to dinner by myself. I never went to the movies alone. We always went out together. I'd like to have a man in my life again.

Widow after widow has written or talked to me about loneliness, both physical and emotional. Most women just miss having someone to share things with, to have a conversation with. Widowhood is not a life sentence in some void, and many women have worked their way through loneliness to have fulfilling relationships once again. In every case the woman who does is one who remains active and who is out there trying to meet new people. In the early stages of widowhood, you probably won't even be interested in dates or sex, but eventually a desire to share life with someone does come back.

Anne Rosberger, executive director of the New York Bereavement and Loss Center, told me, "After the numbness of early grief and with the relentless push of time comes the feeling that the husband who has died is not returning. No matter how you pray, or bargain, or plead, you cannot turn back the clock. It's finished. At that point most widows come to a downward slope, a period of depression and a lack of interest in things that formerly caused pleasure. Sex goes out the window. At that time most widows are too self-involved to be aware of their bodies' needs. It's more of a 'please-hold-me'-type feeling, not 'let's get together sexually.' But as they begin to realize that death has occurred, that their husbands are not retrievable, that they will be going on alone, then there is an awakening of sexual need."

I was married to Martin for seventeen years. Martin was ill for fourteen months, in and out of the hospital before dying of cancer. We had enjoyed a good sex life during our marriage, and when I became aware of my own reemerging sexual needs, I wanted to resume having a good sex life. But where was the person I would have this good sex life with? How was I supposed to find someone? I wanted sex, but I didn't want *just* sex. Along with sex, I wanted companionship, warmth, someone to share good times with, and love, and I had little idea how to find all that. The social and sexual rules and morality had changed while I was married, and I honestly was very unsure of how to behave.

We were childhood sweethearts for ten years before our twelve-year marriage. I could say he was my only love.

In my book *Widow* I talked about some of the ways I tried to answer the question of How? and With whom? Like calling up an old lover who didn't remember who I was. Very humiliating. Or being so nervous with a man that I drank enough vodka martinis to kill a horse and spent a good part of the evening vomiting in the bathroom.

I had been used to men who pursued women, but I wasn't being pursued the way I remembered it. Before I married Martin, I was a potential wife. I didn't have to present myself as some kind of sexual bombshell or great lover. I didn't have to be everything all at once. Things seemed to move more slowly. We dated for a while and took the time to get to know each other. Widowhood today really drops you into another world.

The current state of sexuality in our society is not much comfort to a widow who has come from a different social scene. A poll of more than a thousand men and women aged eighteen to sixty was conducted by New York University a few years ago. It was discovered that their greatest source of stress came from changes in society's attitudes toward sex, including permissiveness and the new social roles of the sexes. If that same poll were taken today, I've no doubt the greatest source of stress would be AIDS.

I've been a widow for two years and felt completely out of it when I started dating again. I didn't know what to say or how to act. Besides, there's no such thing as a date anymore, it's all a long one-night stand. I wanted my husband back, someone who knew me, who understood me. The thought of starting from square one was terrifying to me.

You'd think that dating would be easier when you're a widow. You've had experience with men, or at least one man. You know how to carry on a conversation. You've been in bed with a man before. You're not an inexperienced kid anymore. A point that all widows seem to agree on is that dating and sexual relationships don't get easier when you're a widow. The truth is it's difficult for everybody, and one reason is that sex and dating are no longer separate issues. If you're dating, you're facing the question of sex, and if you're thinking about dating, you will have to deal with it sooner rather than later. A widow recently told me that she had dated two men since her husband died, and both of them were very open about the fact that they felt safe with her because she'd been married for so long to one man. She hadn't been out in the social scene and exposed to AIDS, and they were relieved.

No one can promise that you will meet someone, fall in love, and live happily ever after. I certainly can't. But you can have a life again; you can enjoy sharing things with someone again. I can't say how long a relationship will last or give you ten sure ways to meet the man of your dreams. They don't exist as far as I'm concerned. But I know a lot about what you can do because I've learned from trial and error, and many widows have given me insights through their experiences.

Lately I've had to stifle the urge to deck every divorcée I meet and then ask for the address of her "ex." I'm getting desperate.

FORGET ABOUT THE RULES

Be the exception to the rule. It is a fact that there are many more available women than men, so it would seem that the odds are stacked against you. Statistics are always reminding us of that. If you believe it, they will be. Forget about the odds. You are not a statistic, you're an individual. Don't let yourself be defeated before you even try.

I was really fed up with myself yesterday. I'm tired of loneliness and I'm tired of not seeing any way out of it. I'd like to have a man in my life again.

ARRANGED DATING

You probably have not even thought about a blind date since high school or college; maybe you never have. It's time now to consider it

246

seriously. Your friends and relatives know people who know people, and there just might be someone in that network you should meet.

There is a silly stigma attached to blind dates that implies an inability on your part to get a date. That's a lot of garbage. There are a number of things in favor of blind, or arranged, dating. You have some idea in advance of whom you are meeting. You can ask questions about a man your friend suggests for you. Has he been married? Does he have children? What are his main interests? You can confidentially ask things that would be difficult to bring up on a first or even second date. And you can assume that your friend is answering general questions about you, too. Both of you approach your first meeting with enough information to know that you'd like to get together and that you have something to talk about, even if it's just about the fact that you have a mutual friend. You can also expect that your feelings will be considered with greater sensitivity by your date than by a man you just picked up somewhere. And you'll be more comfortable knowing that your date is liked and respected by a friend.

Certainly, blind dates don't always work

out, and it's probably a good idea not to make it an evening get-together in case it's dislike on sight. Your friend's taste in men may not be the same as yours. You may simply not be attracted to him, or he to you. But when you're ready, you should let the people around you know that you'd like to meet someone. You might be delightfully surprised, and that possibility makes it worth the effort.

For a long time, I felt as if I had had shock treatments, and then the feeling started to come back. Our sex life was good, and it's difficult now to be without it. But worse, what am I going to do without the talk— those long hours in the evening in winter poking the fire and in the summer on the patio? And yet the idea of dating terrifies me.

DATING SERVICES

Women and men are turning to video and computer dating services in big numbers. They're no longer seen as a desperate measure on the part of some socially unacceptable person, but are considered a respectable way of meeting people. Dating services are big business, and they got that way for one reason: They're successful. Although statistics vary, some agencies report a 10 percent to 20 percent marriage rate and 30 percent to 40 percent rate of serious and steady relationships. Dating services attract people of all ages, backgrounds, and professions.

There are lots of different types of services, and you should shop around to find the one that suits you. With the video services you make the choice of who you'd like to meet, based on biographical information and viewings of videotaped interviews. Other dating agencies work by monthly newsletters that list a brief description of clients. If you're interested, you receive a more in-depth bio, and then you can be in touch by phone or mail before meeting.

There are even special-interest services that cater to art or music lovers and people with specific religious affiliations. (Perhaps someone will start one for widows and widowers.) And there are matchmaking services that have someone else do the choosing for you.

Here are a couple of tips on using these services: Before you try a dating service, check it out with the Better Business Bureau. And if you find someone you'd like to know better, set up your first meeting in a public place during the day, not in your home.

DAYTIME DATES

There is no rule that says a date has to take place at night. An evening get-together can put extra pressure on you. Ending the evening with a new person can be awkward when you're just starting to date again. Should you invite him in for coffee? Should you say good-night at the front door? What if he invites you back to his house for a drink? Should you go? There is a very simple way to eliminate these and other questions that you face at the end of a nighttime date. Make it a daytime date. If someone asks you to dinner and you're not comfortable, say you're busy, but suggest brunch on Sunday, a trip to a museum or the zoo, or an afternoon cup of coffee. A movie or matinee is not the best idea. It requires your attention and doesn't give you the opportunity to get to know one another. Save that kind of date for later. And it's a wonderful idea for you to take an active part in setting up a meeting place or an activity. What would *you* like to do?

When you do feel comfortable enough to go out for an evening dinner, but not comfortable enough for it to go further, you can still make suggestions that will not put anyone under pressure. If he invites you to his house for an after-dinner drink, suggest another place where you can be on common ground—a café or even a diner for coffee. Remember that the word "no" can be a complete sentence. You don't have to put yourself in a situation you're not comfortable with or ready for.

MAKING FRIENDS

There is nothing wrong with having men friends with whom you have no romantic involvement. When you join groups or activities, you may meet men who just fall into the category of pal, rather than partner. It's important to have men friends, and I encourage women not to reject a possible friendship just because someone doesn't look like a prospective lover or husband. Male friends can help you relearn about men. They can help you to become comfortable again in the company of a man. And because there are fewer demands put on both of you, these relationships tend to be more open and balanced and mutually beneficial. It also gives you the chance to meet *his* friends.

I think many women really crave companionship in order to get back into the mainstream of going to movies or out to dinner with someone—a man. Just having the facade of being part of a couple enables you to enter the couple's world.

I think the point of enlarging your circle of friends—men and women—is to build a foundation from which you can branch out and create your own network of social opportunities.

I flirted with a rich bachelor friend of Fred's at the house after the funeral. That sounds terrible, and I felt very guilty about it. But when I met a young widow who became a friend, she told me that at first she, too, was obsessed with finding someone to take care of her. Later she gained confidence in herself and stopped screwing around with people who never had any intention of helping her.

LOOKING FOR
THE WRONG REASONS

Don't get caught up in trying to enlarge your circle of friends for the purpose of increasing your bank account. It never works out.

There were times when I worried so much about money that I would have gone out with Godzilla if he had shown up on the first of the month with the rent check. Godzilla never showed up with the rent, and neither did anyone else. I was looking for a man out of desperation, and I know now that it wasn't a very positive motive for wanting someone. But the real issue wasn't money, although it was truly a source of worry. I was acting out of fear. There's always a negative payoff when you try to use somebody instead of doing something for yourself. My negative payoff was that I wasted a lot of time waiting for someone to bail me out, rather than doing what needed to be done. The ultimate positive message is that adversity makes you grow. We all have more resources than we're aware of, and I had to learn to use mine. If you go out into the world looking for a meal ticket, you'll probably be disappointed. People sense when they're being sized up—"My children need a father and money in the bank." "I wonder if I could ask him to fix the hot-water heater."—and no one likes it. You're putting extra pressure on everyone when you set yourself up that way.

I finally got used to paying the monthly rent myself and found I was a lot more relaxed in social situations because of it. Instead of trying to hook myself up with a meal ticket, I relied on myself, and it was a lot more fun.

If you step out and accept the opportunity for growth and positive change, then wonderful things can happen.

I met Prince Charming last year—sure that this relationship was going to save me from being alone and provide a father for my children. However, after eight months, Prince Charming turned out to be not so charming.

KEEPING THINGS IN PERSPECTIVE

It is very easy when you're lonely and vulnerable to start imagining that your childhood fairy tales are true. I remember a widow from California who told me that she had just met the most terrific man. He was handsome, rich, intelligent, an all-around Mr. Wonderful who was falling in love with her. She thought that all her troubles would be over soon. I shouldn't have been surprised that her daydream bore an uncanny resemblance to some of my own and to those of many other widows I've met. Even if she had found the gallant knight of her dreams, how could he possibly have lived up to those expectations? She wrote to me later to say that just about the only thing that turned out to be true in her relationship with this man was that he really was handsome.

I want to meet someone fabulous and live happily ever after.

If you fill yourself with fantasies of perfection, you're headed for a fall. When you're dating someone new, you're both getting to know each other. It's a good time to put your expectations in check until you know more.

I've given affairs some thought, but I have so many strikes against me. Could I respond to anyone after inhibiting my sexual feelings for so long? I don't know.

Would I become sexually permissive? I've never really known another man intimately, and I don't know how I would react. Would I freeze? Underneath my clothes is a body that has borne children. Would a man find me repulsive? Dare I take a chance and find out? I'm a coward when it comes to taking a chance on rejection. I not only have a hysterectomy scar, I also have very bad stretch marks. How would a man feel about that?

It never ceases to amaze me how generous widows are in sharing their experiences with other widows. During the question-and-answer sessions I hold after speaking engagements and seminars, widows always teach and help each other by talking about their own lives. They speak about sexuality with great honesty.

We all face the same world out there, but each woman has her own approach to fulfilling needs for sex or companionship. Some women continue active sex lives or have temporary alliances. Others leave sex behind forever and in place of it sublimate or masturbate. Their reasons vary from a desire to uncomplicate their lives to the fear of AIDS that hangs over everyone. You have to find the way that is right for you, and I don't think anyone can really tell you what that is. But it can be enormously helpful to hear about the challenges other widows have faced and how they responded.

I was forty-five years old when my husband died of cancer. He was sick for over two-years and was unable to have sex during the last year and a half. That was OK with me. Full of sorrow and fear, sex was the last thing on my mind. But after he died, all of my repressed sexual feelings began to surface.

I had been married and remained faithful for twenty two years and was unprepared for the new attitudes about sex that prevailed: Men expecting you to put out on the first date, and not calling again if you didn't. And sometimes not calling if you did. No courtship. No tenderness. Sexual etiquette had completely changed in twenty-two years. I felt as if I were on another planet, but I kept dating because my friends said it was good for me and that it was the only way to get over my grief. Since I had been accustomed to a good sex life, I had very strong urges. However, they remained unfulfilled. You see, I was also unprepared for the high incidence of impotence among men over forty.

The first man I went to bed with—well-mannered everywhere but in the bedroom—blamed me for his inability to perform and insisted that I satisfy him orally; help him, as he put it. Yuck. I didn't even like it with my own husband, whom I was crazy about. But I was so afraid to be without a man, that I did anything to please him. The only way I could do it was to heavily fortify myself with liquor.

Eventually, I did meet a man who at least knew how to talk to a woman. He was impotent, too, most of the time, but what he lacked in virility he made up for in sweet talk. From the start I knew he was extremely disturbed and mean-spirited, but he was a distinguished archaeologist and I considered myself fortunate to have him in my life. Seeking carnal oblivion, I went along with what became a very kinky relationship. The only way he could have an erection—which he could rarely sustain—was by talking dirty and engaging in degrading sexual fantasies in which I was either a whore, a relative, or his mother, sister, or daughter. In my effort to please him, I even wore costumes. You should have seen me decked out in a pinafore, white silk knee socks, and Mary Janes, with my hair tied back with a blue satin bow. Ten pounds overweight and forty-four yet.

After a year or so, the relationship played itself out. Today, I'm embarrassed when I think about it. Sex is the most superficial kind of intimacy.

SINGLES BARS

One place I absolutely *don't* recommend for meeting someone is a bar. There aren't many places really set up for women to be in the company of men they feel comfortable with. There's a lot of disease around. There's AIDS, there's herpes. There are many more fears today about meeting someone. Suppose he's on drugs, or suppose he gets violent. The newspapers are full of frightening accounts of women who got tangled up in bad situations.

Singles bars can be dangerous, and none of us are seeking some casual encounter. No matter your age, a bar is a rotten place to look for a man. I think most of us want the kind of sex that is built on a warm and affectionate relationship. It's hard enough to find, but you certainly aren't going to find it in a singles bar. Widowhood erodes your self-esteem. You've lost not only your husband, but your status and probably your life-style. You do not need to lose your self-respect on top of all that.

I had sex for the first time about a year and a half after Edward's death. I wanted to make sure that I was still alive. Maybe I wanted to know if I could still do it. At least I found out that I could still do the mechanical things, like getting undressed in front of someone, and that I didn't burst into tears when he touched me. I wondered if I could have an orgasm. I couldn't. I was too busy watching and waiting to put my arms around myself if I began to cry. There was no intimacy. He couldn't give me what I needed; to hug me so I wouldn't have to hug myself. I wasn't in love. I wasn't even in like. I considered him an experiment. At least I allowed someone to come close and I took my clothes off.

CASUAL SEX

The one-night stand doesn't work for most women. Men no longer need to commit to a relationship because they can have almost anyone they want sexually. Some widows decide to have no sex rather than taking on the rotten feeling the "day after" can give you. It's like eating chocolate cake when you're trying to take off weight. You feel great while you're doing it, but the day after can leave you full of disgust. As a married woman, you were used to having a man care about you sexually, accustomed to intimacy and sex with a man who had feelings for you. After the first careless rapture of a casual encounter, what's left for you? He doesn't call again. You're still alone, probably feeling even more alone than before. If this is your reaction to casual sex, recreational sex, and one-night stands, you should probably steer clear of them.

I had one lovely experience in Chicago with a journalist who interviewed me for a newspaper. I knew him from my work in publicity, setting up book tours for other authors, but we had never spent any time together socially. He called me up after the interview and asked me to have dinner with him. He was a charming, attractive, and considerate man. He came to my hotel, we had a lovely dinner together, and he spent the night with me. The next morning he said, "I always feel very tender toward a woman I have enjoyed spending the night with, and I wonder if there is anything I can do for you." I thought that was wonderful. He drove me to the outskirts of the city, where I had to drop off some autographed copies of *Widow*, and we had a late breakfast together. It was just a beautiful, off-the-map experience with a gentle, sensitive man. We stayed in touch as friends for a long time after that, but the distance between our home cities prevented it from going further.

Maybe this was just a nice exception to the usual one-night stand, and this man was certainly not a stranger. I think that when the people are right and the circumstances are right, there is nothing wrong with a relationship that doesn't have a future. When both people walk away feeling good, having gained something from the encounter, the experience can have a positive effect on you.

My talks with widows are full of stories of casual sex that led to unhappy feelings. Not all my experiences were great either. I think

262

that anyone can have sex, if that's all you want and if you're willing to set your standards low enough. But how you feel afterward, the day after, a week after, is a good indication of whether or not recreational sex is healthy for you. Some women I talked to found casual sex to be a positive experience. They really didn't want strings and didn't feel ready for a relationship. It was more a question of whether or not they were still able to do it. Most said they were unable to have an orgasm, but knowing that they could take their clothes off in front of someone and be touched without falling apart gave them what they needed from the experience. In the case of casual sex, I think you have to let your own feelings guide you. If you don't feel good afterward, then you're probably better off not getting involved just for the sake of sex.

I cannot live in loneliness and without love for always, so if I ever do find another love, it will be more selfless and more infinite because my husband left the better part of himself with me.

AFFAIRS OF THE HEART

It's interesting to me that the word "affair" (which comes from the French *a faire*, meaning "to do") was originally used in terms of business or politics (affairs of state) and referred to a professional interaction between men. It had nothing to do with love or sex or women. Sometime around the eighteenth century, the definition expanded a little to include a short romantic relationship. It still carried a business connotation though, and I guess that's because at the time a respectable woman didn't have an affair, unless it was a business proposition. Certainly there were people who had love affairs that had nothing to do with business, but it's fascinating that the language of the time didn't even offer a way to express such an alliance. How far we've come, thank God!

The decision of whether affairs are right or wrong for you is a personal one. I certainly can't make such a choice for you, but I think that affairs are healthy. If you're lucky enough to find a warm and sensitive man, the affair can be joyous. A good one has the power to pull you out of despair, even if just temporarily. An affair can turn into a marriage or a friendship—or at least a pleasant memory.

Of course, the other side of the coin is that affairs end, but even with an awkward or painful ending, I wouldn't give up the affairs I've had. They were fun, difficult, infuriating, exhilarating, sad, and passionate, and they made me feel *alive*.

My husband was much older than I, and though sex had been good with us, it didn't happen often. Perhaps not often enough to satisfy my stronger needs, but I had sublimated this. Before my husband died suddenly, at the beginning of the summer, we had arranged with good friends Jim and Edna, a long-married professional couple, to spend the weekend at our country house. After the sudden death, they called and assumed I would cancel the date. "You come to us," Edna said. "Let us take care of you. Just rest. You don't need the work of having guests."

I was in a state of complete shock and didn't want to leave the familiar house. I remember saying on the phone, "Please come here. I would like to have somebody to cook for."

They came, and that was the beginning of this very gentle, sweet, intelligent man's wooing me with great understanding. He did not force himself on me in any way. The whole summer is misty. I must have been very much in need of love, or what passed for love, or what I called love and sex. The sex was absolutely wonderful—I remember that—better than my beloved husband had been for a long time. I think it helped me a great deal in wooing me back into this world. I don't think his wife knew—not in the beginning, at least—but as it turned out, for many years he'd had affairs with many different women, and his wife had accepted it. He was very sweet and gentle, as well as brilliant, witty, charming. It was truly a beautiful interlude that helped me over this terrible time.

YOUR CHANGING BODY

I've written about my own embarrassment of being in a sexual situation with a man and being extremely uptight because I didn't shave my legs and that the birth of one of my children by cesarean caused a road-map scar on my stomach and that my thighs were somewhat heavier than they were twenty years ago. I learned that I am not alone. Anne Rosberger of the Bereavement and Loss Center of New York explained, "Their husbands saw them in their early days when they were firm and lovely. Even if they were heavy, they had young bodies. As you go along, whatever happens, happens to husband and wife together. You change together. Then, suddenly, new eyes, fresh eyes are looking at your body. It's like someone new coming to your home, and suddenly you realize your exercise bike is sitting in the living room, where it shouldn't be. It seems like part of the furniture to you, but you realize that to someone new it looks rather strange there."

A widow friend of mine described what I think qualifies as a record for insensitive remarks. A man she was in bed with said of her cesarean scar, "I could kill the butcher who mutilated your beautiful body." How's that for a confidence builder? The ironic thing is she told me that he would have won, thumbs up, any election for the president of the One Inch Club.

There's no question that an aging man is more sexually acceptable than an aging woman. In our society, a man can have a potbelly, gray hair, a caved-in chest, and flat feet, and that's all OK. It's not right, it's not fair, but that's the way it is.

I was sexually dead for at least five years after Dick died. It was so sudden. He went jogging in the park one morning and never came back. We had a very solid marriage. I was so devastated that I really wasn't interested in men. I also felt that I would be betraying Dick, committing spiritual adultery. But I was used to a satisfying sex life and began to get very horny. When my friend Helen fixed me up with a lawyer who was separated from his wife, I went straight to bed with him the very first night. He wore a hearing aid and had a game leg, but his other parts worked just fine. Afterward, I removed my husband's photographs from the bedroom, and I've been sexually active ever since.

I have been ostracized. I was only thirty-seven at the time, and I really went crazy. My husband was terminally ill for two years. I never thought about another man. There was a lot of trouble over a married man who came to my house the day my husband died. He brought his wife and children with him (that time!). I was in another world in those days. I never even thought why he was around so much. Then a few months later he kissed me. I hadn't been really kissed since my husband first became ill. I almost swooned. After that, I didn't care what people thought, though I was careful around my children. Well, after that blew up and everybody found out about it, there were people on my side and people on the side of the man's wife. His wife doesn't want him anymore, and he doesn't want me. What a mess.

ALCOHOL, DRUGS, AND SEX

Excessive alcohol does not go well with sex— or with anything else. Many widows tell me that in order to be involved in sexual situations they have to drink to relax and rid themselves of inhibitions. Widowhood can make you feel desperate and full of pain, and alcohol or drugs can create a feeling of oblivion or abandon. But neither alcohol nor drugs really reduce fear or pain or make a very stable stepping-stone to a positive sexual relationship. If you have to drink or drug yourself through something, what you're doing probably isn't right for you.

I was so terrified of being alone that I forced myself to go out with men I didn't like. I thought anything would be better than feeling like I was going crazy from loneliness. To get through some of those miserable dates, I'd take a couple of drinks before I went out. Then I'd have a drink before dinner, and maybe a couple with dinner, and one or two after dinner. That whole period of my life is a big blur. I'm sure I'd be embarrassed if I could remember what happened. I finally stopped when I woke up one morning on the living room floor with a man who was a complete stranger to me. I had no recollection how I got there or who he was. That was the end of drinking for me.

FINDING OTHER OUTLETS

What about the widows who, for whatever reason, no longer include sex as part of their lives. What happens to them once thoughts or feelings about sex become a thing of the past?

After everything is over and once some semblance of sanity returns—then you remember things, really unbelievable things. For instance, I remember that while I was sitting in the hospital corridor waiting for the doctor, a friend of my husband said to me, "What are you going to do about your sex life? After all, you're still a young woman." My first instinct was to say, "Masturbate, you idiot." How I wish I'd said that. Instead, I looked at the floor and said nothing.

I asked Anne Rosberger about this, because it's a subject she deals with very often. "Many widows give up having sex, but they find other ways of releasing their sexual energy. Masturbation is a very important aspect for many women. For most it's still a no-no. They just never learned how to masturbate, so now when they need to relieve sexual tension they have no way to do it, and it's very sad. So we teach them how to give themselves pleasure. At first they're very shy, embarrassed, disquieted by it. They're ashamed to say they've never done it or that

271

they'll try. But we teach them, show them vibrators, and explain the use of them and how they can even play a part in the relationship of couples.

"At first some of them are bewildered. But once they try masturbation, they report that it felt good. It doesn't take the place of a real sexual encounter, and no one claims that it does. It's simply a way of reducing the tension, the sense of isolation, and the sense of being denied something that one should be able to have. As one widow said, 'I know my husband died. I didn't die. And I am still left with these needs.'"

I can recommend what I think is an excellent book on female sexuality, *For Yourself* by Lonnie Garfield Barbach (New American Library/Signet, 1976). It's full of down-to-earth, supportive, educational information on sexual self-fulfillment.

There are other ways women are fulfilling their needs. A publishing colleague of mine told me a story about a high-powered executive in a large company who exhibited the most unattractive macho qualities, was loud and emotionally abusive to those who worked with and for him. Most of his business associates couldn't stand him. He was married to a lovely, quiet, attractive woman, who must have loved him. I don't know how she could have stayed with him otherwise. And then, one day, she left him.

She left him for another woman.

I'm telling this story because I think it happens more than many of us realize. This woman was not a widow. She had a husband and yet left him to go live with a woman. I've encountered this kind of situation among widows, too. They say, in most cases, that they like men, and they miss having a man around. But they are unable to get from other men what they need—nurturing, companionship, warmth, closeness—and there were always strings attached to everything. I don't imagine there are any statistics on this, but I've heard enough personal stories to know that it does happen. Maybe it has to do with there being too many women and not enough men or with the way men and women treat each other today. Maybe it has something to do with the sexual freedom we've enjoyed over the past twenty years. I don't have the answer.

I became a widow at the age of thirty-two. My husband was fifty-six when he died of cancer. We were both entertainers. He managed my career and the rest of my life as well.

There I was, a young widow who had been married to someone who cared about me a great deal. I felt as though I were in a nightmare, an absolute nightmare. I went to bed with a man only three weeks after he died. I was still in shock, didn't know what planet I was on. The man was a former lover. What a mistake it was. It was like I wasn't there. I was watching my body go through these motions, but I wasn't there. It wasn't a good experience.

Six months later, when the fog started to lift, I had another ghastly experience. He was an old friend of mine, a man in his late thirties who had been married twice. He was so coarse, so insensitive, so selfish, and had premature ejaculations to boot. I even asked him, "Have you ever been to bed with a woman before?" He didn't care in the least about satisfying me. I was absolutely amazed that men had not changed while I was married, during the early seventies and the sexual revolution. This man knew nothing about female sensibility, female orgasm, the whole female scope. He was out of tune and out of touch.

Finally, I did find someone I liked, but it was a case of the right person at the wrong time. Charles was coming out of a divorce at the same time I was coming out of a death. He was a lovely man, extremely kind and sensitive, and he really loved women. I think very few men like women at all, and I think Charles was one of the exceptions. But he was living in California, and I was living in New York. I had finally found an apartment and was still settling in. I had just started therapy and was unwilling to uproot myself again. When Ted died I lost my house and had to move out of my community in order to make a living. Now that I was back on my feet, I just couldn't pick up and go to California. I didn't know anyone there and had no support system except Charles. I just couldn't do it. He's married now, and I'll always care about him and be grateful for his loving support during that terrible time of early widowhood.

I went into therapy with a woman and continued there for three and a half years. There was an empathy that we had with each other that I felt. I didn't know anything about her personal life, but I felt that whatever I brought up, she knew exactly what I was talking about. I found out she had experienced many of the same things I did; the same hardships, the same predicaments. And she was always there for me. On many nights I called her in the middle of the night, and she'd stay on the phone with me for hours. Very unusual for a therapist you may be sure.

I developed an attraction for her that grew stronger and stronger. I thought we'd have to end the therapy, but we talked it through, thought we had resolved it, and then went on with therapy for another year. We were sexually attracted to one another, but understood that we were in a client-therapist relationship and that seeing each other outside the session was against the rules. But the attraction came up again, and then it wasn't fine anymore, and we couldn't go on with the therapy. We ended that relationship and started seeing each other socially. Today we're living together and we're lovers. We are very devoted to each other, and I get the nurturing, caring, and the emotional support that I couldn't find with a man. I had that with my husband, but I just couldn't seem to find it with a man after he died.

She's divorced with two children and was married for almost twenty years. Neither of us particularly feel that we are lesbians. To me, a lesbian is a woman whose orientation is totally homosexual. We don't relate to that type of gay woman, and we don't fit into the gay world.

I felt that we should tell her children—they're teenagers, a boy and a girl—but she didn't agree. She feels that they know what's going on and when they're ready to really deal with it, they'll bring it up. We certainly don't flaunt it, but we do sleep in the same bed. They understand that we're very important to each other.

Given today's divorce rate and the dearth of men, it might well be that more and more women will seek each other. I don't advocate lesbianism. I think it's very difficult because it's not the norm. It's harder for two women together to make a living. A man makes more money.

I think it would be a lot easier to be with a man, but I'm not. I don't know if I'll ever be with a man again. I miss it sometimes. I miss men sexually and in other ways, too. But I have a deep commitment to Margaret, and that's the way it is. I'm happy now. This is the first good relationship I've had since my husband died. So it's not male or female, it's really the person. I feel that I'm totally accepted, good or bad. I felt that with my husband, too. With everybody in between there have always been conditions. "I'll love you if you can be this for me or if you can do that for me." Unconditional love is hard to find, gay or straight.

Unless there is a definite outlet for sexuality, unless there is someone to whom a widow is attached for at least a period of time, it seems that for the majority of women, sexuality is put to rest. They do various things to sublimate. By sublimation I don't mean repression, but rechanneling, of sexual energy. They're involved with putting that energy into their family or some other pastime. It is getting more frightening for widows who have many lovers or one-night stands because of so many social problems we face—disease, violence, insensitivity. It's no longer that easy to feel emotionally or physically safe having sex with strangers, and the artificial intimacies are wearing thin. Many widows just eliminate sex from their lives.

I had to learn all over again about dating and sex after Martin died, and I made plenty of mistakes that caused me unhappiness. But apparently I did a few things right, because I've also had plenty of wonderful and loving moments. It took a long time for me to trust my own feelings and intuition about what was right or wrong for me, but time and time again that proved to be the key to making choices about the men in my life.

12

THE NEW YOU

Dear Lynn

Eight years ago, my husband died of liver cancer, leaving me with three children, ages eight, ten, and twelve. Luckily, I had a job. My family and I did not have an easy time. The financial problems were very real. It took a while, but I pulled myself out of a large debt and bought a new home and a new car. I'm back in school myself working toward a degree in education. I've worked hard. My children are older now and very independent. They had to learn to be on their own a lot in those early days after Barry died, and I don't regret that they are able to take care of themselves. One of them is in college at the same time I am! I'm proud of the adjustment we have all made, and I feel that because of our love for each other we will continue to do fine. I feel that we have weathered a storm. I can even say that I am content now and that I like the different "me." I remember my husband often and will always love him. I have been able to go on, but I will never forget. Life really is getting better all the time. I learned that courage and perseverance will always see me through no matter what happens.

"I am a widow who is no longer maudlin, crazed, or chaotic, but emerged from grief. I am a woman who lost her husband but found herself. I had a hard time of it at first, but I can now say that I like who I am and that I'm proud of what I have accomplished. I am not just a survivor. I am a different person, a new person, better and stronger than I was before."

Those words are from a speech I made in Los Angeles. If anyone had told me at the time of Martin's death that years later I would be able to say such things and mean them, I would not have believed it. I was shattered, so frightened of what was going to happen to me, that I often went to bed praying I wouldn't wake up the next morning. Very slowly those feelings began to pass, and I found that the life urge in me was stronger than the death urge. I decided that I would live with as much grace, joy, and fulfillment as I possibly could. It took time and work, *hard* work.

Someone recently asked me if there had been a moment, a turning point I could remember, that was a catalyst for that decision. Actually, there were many such moments. There was a first night in I don't know how long that I slept through until morning without waking up in a panic. There was a first time I could remember Martin with love instead of with anger and hate. And, most important, there was a first time I realized that Jon and Elizabeth and I were still a family and that I cherished them. But there was an incident I wrote about in *Lifelines* that provided a great personal opportunity for change.

We were living in a suburb in New Jersey at the time, and I felt isolated, out of my element, and miserable. I was commuting into the city each day to my job as publicity director for a publisher. I was planning to move back into New York and had just made the preliminary overtures to friends and real estate agents to find us an apartment. That's when this wonderful and terrifying opportunity presented itself.

A close friend of mine who was producing

Barbara Walters's network program *Not for Women Only* called to tell me that the staff was planning a three-week series on birth, marriage, and death.

"I need a woman panelist for the death show. I have an internist, a psychiatrist, a minister . . ." Julie said nervously.

"Great, what can I do to help?"

"Come on the show, *please*," she begged. "I'm really stuck, and I need someone fast."

I was in shock. I'd never been on television, but I wanted to help a good friend. I also had a strong sense that a door was opening for me. After taking a night to sleep on it, I called Julie back and agreed to appear. I could never have imagined where that decision would lead me.

Barbara Walters is such a canny interviewer that I found myself discussing Martin's death and its aftermath and saying things on network television that I hadn't admitted to anyone. I talked about how I was angry at Martin for abandoning me and for leaving us with no money and said that my children were small comfort. I talked about how overwhelmed I was, how lonely, and how I missed sex. And I talked about how I felt betrayed by our closest friends. On and on I went.

"I want Lynn Caine to keep talking," Ms.

Walters said. "She's the only member of the panel who has had a recent direct experience with death."

I was on with her for the entire week.

Never underestimate the power of television. Four publishers and two literary agents who had watched the show called me during the next few days. "You have to write a book about your experience," they said. "There is nothing available on what it's like to be a widow in America."

With that kind of encouragement, I got down to work with the journals I'd written. I called them my paper psychiatrist. Some of them were so awful, so ugly, that I had burned them so my children would never read them. But I had kept dozens of notebooks. The only outlet I had for my emotions—my nocturnal scrawls—became the raw material for *Widow*. The book was very well received and certainly changed my life. I found out how unprepared I was for instant minicelebrity status, and that brought a new set of problems to deal with. But there were rewards. It eased my financial situation and also served as a catharsis. Preparing the book forced me to confront my grief because I had to go over the experience again and again. It forced me to feel, and I think that was the true turning point.

The publication of *Widow* put me on a path that has ultimately led to this book and gave me many other wonderful experiences in between. One of those has been hearing from widows who have told me *their* personal stories of triumph over the adversity that widowhood brings. It happens that the crisis a woman faces in recovering from the loss of her husband may be the greatest opportunity for self-exploration that she has ever experienced in her life. It's interesting to note that of the two Chinese characters used for the word "crisis," the first one means danger and the second means opportunity. It's true. The shock of widowhood produces a make-it-or-break-it situation, but may provide a tremendous release in which women can build new lives that are even more self-expressive, fulfilling, rewarding and happy. With that thought, I want to turn this chapter over to some of those women. I want you to hear how other widows have forged new identities and discovered new selves. Their stories are a celebration of and testament to the opportunity for growth and change that can be positive and joyful.

DISCOVERING INDEPENDENCE

"I felt in some ways that my husband had created me, and in a great many respects he had. My parents were not the kind to lavish a great deal on a child. They felt that if they clothed you, and fed you, and kept a roof over your head, that was really sufficient. My husband was the one who gave me wonderful things, mainly the time and the ability to develop into something.

"I had always felt so independent. I thought that I was so great and so smart and actually operating on my own, when all the time I wasn't. I was backed up by my husband. There was a basis, a foundation. His death was like the bottom of the triangle falling off. I felt that he had created me, and without him there, the creation just disappeared in some way. After he died, I realized that I was a lot less secure and a lot less independent than I thought. I was frightened. I also had to face a lot of harsh realities. For the first time in my life, I was out of work. My career was floundering badly. I had some money, but I was terrified to spend it. I remember once saying to myself, 'I'm going to give myself a treat today. I'm going to buy a steak.' It was so silly. I could well afford it, but I thought carefully about every dollar I spent. It was an awful feeling.

"I got myself back into the fashion world, which was my business, and immersed myself in work. I felt it would be my only way out. My job had always given me pleasure, and I just focused on it and held on to it for dear life. It wasn't only the money it brought in, but the way it made me feel. It's a cliché, I guess, but I felt proud of myself.

"I have a new relationship with a man now, and that's different, too. I treat him so differently that it makes me feel guilty. I am so much nicer to him. I'm so much more loving and supportive. I think I appreciate him more because I found out what it's like to really feel alone. But I think about where I'm going with this man. I don't want to be involved in a live-in situation. I don't believe in it for me. I'm too old for that. I don't need a boyfriend. I would like to have a husband again. But he has children, he has sons-in-law, he has grandchildren. It's not just him, but the whole package, and I don't want to be put in a funny situation. It's as though I will now be giving up yet another identity—the one I worked so hard for—and starting in again. I'm used to being alone and doing everything *I* want. So once again, it's an adjustment.

"I also feel afraid with him sometimes. If he coughs, I'm sure it's tuberculosis. If he has a headache, I'm sure it's a brain tumor. I've become a little paranoid. It's almost funny. I'm older now. I know things can work out, and I know some things don't. I also know that a husband can die. When you marry the first time you're sure that everything is going to be so wonderful. It's going to be like an MGM musical. I know now that the movies are the movies and life is life. I'm older and I've been alone, and when I say 'I love you' now it means more than it used to.

"Based on what I know from experience, I think widows really have to build a life for themselves. You have to meet people. I think having one overriding interest, no matter what it is—if it's a stamp collection, you go to all the stamp fairs. If it's gardening, you go to all the gardening shows. Whatever it is, you meet people who have the same interests and you build relationships around those interests. Starting a new life may never include a new husband. On the other hand, you can have a very nice life without a husband. I know that. There's a wonderful world out there, but you have to go out and find it. You have to psych yourself up. After a while it gets easier. It's the doing that's important. That's the only thing that will take you where you want to go."

A SHINING LIGHT

"My husband died suddenly and unexpectedly of a heart attack. We had shared a career some years before, but I had been 'at home' for the past five years. We shared every aspect of our lives together. I knew the people he worked with and the details of the business, and we discussed that daily, as we had when I was working. With him gone, I was in a kind of numb shock. I moved around and acted like a normal person, but it was almost as if I were seeing myself walking around in a TV sitcom, eating, dressing, doing chores, etc. I wasn't *there*. I couldn't even cry until some weeks later. Then it happened suddenly, in bed at night, and I sobbed for what seemed like forever.

"My head seemed to me like a dark room. There was no light in it. It didn't hurt. It was just empty and dark. Letters of condolence sort of floated past me. I think I appreciated them, but I didn't really know why or what they were. I just put them in a large pile—there was no possibility that I could have the head to answer them, not until months later. I am basically a strong person and a good healer, practical and realistic, I think. The numbness and 'not being there' was, I think now, a method of letting time heal while I wasn't there—as when we rest and sleep when healing a physical illness or wound. I began to think of my head, which I guess stood for my thinking capacity, as a round dark moon space. I was operating on automatic pilot. Little by little, perhaps beginning by the end of the first month, a thin slit of light, like the beginning of a new moon, opened up. Slowly it became larger, as the moon does each night, and little by little more light, more strength and reason, entered my life. For the first four or five months, the main task of the light was coping with the change in every day—nobody coming home at night for dinner, no one to cook for, no slippers under my bed, and no one to really talk to with the total trust of love. I think those first six months or so were necessary for a kind of emotional healing. I had turned into a different kind of person without him. I had created this cocoon around myself, taking each day as it

290

came and feeling stronger and better, but it wasn't until a woman friend said to me, 'You have to do something. You've got to get out of the house and work. Social life is not enough.' I must have been ready, for as she said it I knew she was right.

"I thought about it, about nothing else, for a few days. I thought about how I had changed . . . no longer a couple. I was just me.

"That wasn't so bad. Yes, it was different. Just how different I would have to learn by venturing out in the world. Looking back, I feel that this was the most important step of all. You have to get out and start again as this new entity, the woman alone. Not bad, not less, just different. And you can't figure out how different or in what way until you get outside the home and operate—at something.

"I had been out of the work force for five years, but had enjoyed a long career before that. I knew that some things had probably happened since I left the business world, and I decided to find out how much. I still had some contacts, and I started with them. I made lunch dates and dinner dates and asked for advice. I found that people like to help, and if you follow up on each and every suggestion, one of them will work and lead you to the right place.

"I did not want to do exactly what I had done before, but I was sensible enough to know that I should find something that used the kind of experience I had, the things I knew. Even if you never worked before, there are some things you do better than others. I think that you have to start with those things."

THE LADY BUILDER

"My husband was twenty years my senior, a retired college professor from a local university. He was a recovering alcoholic. He enjoyed his retirement and did a little consulting work to keep busy and help ends meet. His part-time work didn't do much for our financial situation, and the time came when we needed an additional income. My husband and I built our own home—I acted as contractor—and he knew how much I had enjoyed it. When the money situation got tight, he suggested that I go into the building business for myself, and I did. It was small and new, and I ran around doing it all, and it was a success.

"Two years later he died suddenly. The

funeral was held out of state, and a friend traveled with me to help me through it. When we got back home, she offered to stay the first night so I wouldn't be alone. I thought about it and said, 'Sooner or later I am going to have to get used to sleeping in this house alone, and it might as well be now.' The next day I stayed close to home to take care of notes and condolences and personal business, and five days later I went back to work full steam. The high-pressure job filled my days and gave me hope. I felt my husband had done many things for me and given me many gifts. I never remarried, and being a woman alone is an enormous change I've had to adjust to. Maybe one of the reasons my business has been a success is that as a builder my emphasis has been on 'attention and stroking.' I don't disappear the moment the house is finished. I continue to be available night and day to fix things or take care of whatever is needed. Other builders have families to go home to; being alone gives me more time to devote to my clients. That's earned me a unique reputation as a woman in construction, which is traditionally a man's world.

"I've also always made my decisions carefully. A lot of times I'd ask myself, 'How would my husband do this?' I was careful not to make foolish mistakes. Sometimes thinking, 'Oh, if he could only see me! What would he say now?' Four years after he died, I was elected president of the Home Builders Association. I was the first woman president. It was a big honor, and there was a formal Installation Dinner at which I spoke. I regretted that my husband wasn't there to share it all with me.

"In the seventeen years of our marriage, his devotion to me was unparalleled and his love unconditional. We had grown together to a perfect understanding of our individual identities and roles. Each of us did our thing in a partnership that was free and loving and invincible. I'm sure that special kind of partnership made a difference, because I was able to go on and have a life for myself."

LEARNING TO FLY

"I was alone. That was the main change, in *fact*. What did it do to me? After the initial healing period, getting over the shock and truly knowing that I was alone, I realized that there was something good and rewarding about doing exactly what I wanted to do without asking if someone else approved.

Even finding out what I really wanted was a new challenge. It is almost like creating a new being, a new personality, for a person alone *is* a different personality from the one who is a couple, no matter how loving. I think a truly loving couple can diminish the personality of each, to become together something quite separate. The breaking of such a relationship is very hard, but when it happens and there's no way to go back to it, then it can be turned into a whole new discovery of the new person. Yourself.

"I had a very good marriage for almost twenty years. We were close in every way, even our careers were in the same field. Once when we were on vacation together, I discovered, quite by accident, that I really loved to fly in small airplanes. The trip we were taking required several short hops, and while my husband was turning green in the backseat of a four-seater airplane, I sat up front with the pilot and even took the yoke when he offered to show me how to fly. I had not known that my husband, who was great and happy on big airliners, had this kind of innate fear of little planes. He couldn't help it. When I excitedly said after our flight that I would love to learn and planned to find out where and how when I got back home, he did indeed turn green. He was not the type to forbid his friend and wife to do anything, but it was abundantly clear to me that my learning to fly would have made him extremely nervous and unhappy. So I just forgot about it. One more activity in my life, however challenging, was not worth making him unhappy.

"About ten years after this incident, he died. In the dreadful mourning time that followed, I had the need to fly a short trip to see relatives. I hadn't really flown in a small airplane since that vacation. I was traveling alone, and so I sat again in the front seat with the pilot, and again was allowed to feel the wheel of the plane, to feel the touch that keeps it aloft and heading in the right direction. Since my husband's death a few weeks before, I had been living with what seemed to be a solid bar of pain in my head. It wasn't a headache: It was just a bar that went between my eyes in my head, and it had been there ever since he died. As I took the wheel of the airplane and felt that I was indeed controlling its action, somehow everything in my head and body concentrated on this performance—and the bar of pain disappeared for the first time. Suddenly, I realized that no one was down there worrying about me. When we landed, I asked the pilot about what I needed to do to learn to fly, and that was the beginning of one of the most rewarding experiences in my new life. It added totally new challenges to my days, brought a new kind of person into my life, and the knowledge of the field of aviation that came to me in the months that followed even enhanced my new career.

"I think that as you come out of your grieving you discover that there is someone still inside and that she is different from the partner you were to your husband because there were parts of her that were not used in that relationship. Now independence and self-development come to the fore. I say, let them. Use them. You'll make mistakes and you'll be lonely and wish it were still the old way . . . but get on with it. Action and people are the answers."

EVERY MOMENT COUNTS

"My husband had heart surgery and was home taking it easy, working part time for a while. He ran his own CPA firm and had planned to go back on a full-time schedule in a few days.

"He wasn't feeling well over that weekend, but we went out to a movie and had a little picnic in the park. Monday morning he woke up with a temperature of 103. I canceled a business appointment for him, and a short time later we took his temperature again. It was up to 104. We knew there was something wrong. The doctor met us at the hospital and said they'd run some tests and get the fever down and my husband would probably be sent home the next afternoon.

"I had lunch the next day with an old friend and planned to go up to the hospital afterward. It was while I was having that lunch that my husband went into cardiac arrest and then slipped into a coma. The doctors couldn't understand why it happened. They couldn't find anything wrong with him. He never came out of it, and two weeks later he died.

"I was the only one who was familiar with his CPA business, so I was the one to dispose of it all. I had to call clients and finish up loose ends. It *forced* me to stay in the world. I'd be fine with the clients, very professional and unemotional. But then I'd have to talk to a personal friend or a relative and it would be very difficult for me. Sometimes I'd fall apart and cry. My doctor was concerned about me. She thought I was running away from grief and using the excuse of being busy. But grieving became part of my everyday life. I had to grieve. I just did it in my own way.

"I also had my own typing business to handle. I had started it years before when I was between marriages, mainly to put my daughter through school. It began with typing envelopes: I had a staff of thirteen typists working for me at one time. Then I got into typing manuscripts. It's a good business, and I still run it. So I was wildly busy after he died. I also started an antique-jewelry business, quite by accident. A friend had some stuff she wanted to get rid of, and we wound up doing this flea-market thing. I fell in love with the give-and-take with the people. Slowly we added more and more odds and ends and furniture and finally started to specialize in antique jewelry. It's a big business now, and that's the way I spend my weekends.

"My husband and I were very close. Since we were both self-employed, our schedules could be flexible and we'd see a lot of each other. When he died, there was a blank. I would walk in and think to myself, 'Well I better get dinner started.' Then it would occur to me that I didn't have to have dinner at six o'clock. In fact, I didn't have to have dinner at all if I didn't want to. That overwhelmed me. It was a real sad feeling I had. That was one of the ways I felt my grief. Going to the supermarket was difficult for some reason. I guess because we used to do it together. The little things were difficult, not the restaurants or the movies, but the everyday things would get to me. Some things that I thought would be very difficult for me were actually easy, which I found very strange. For instance, I didn't have a difficult time getting rid of his clothes. But the bag I brought home from the hospital, the one that had his things in it, I couldn't bear to open. I'd just look at it in the closet and close the door. One day I looked at it and got rid of the stuff, but it took me three years to do it.

"Everyone thinks I'm so self-sufficient, and I am. But I don't think I had much choice. It's not by my design, but by my need. I had to work. But I've never been afraid to do things. I think I have more of a fear of not doing things. I find that people build bridges for themselves that they cannot or will not cross. They close doors on themselves.

"There are things I would not have done

if my husband had lived. Certainly, I wouldn't have the antique business. I've enjoyed so many new things, and I've become a lot more selfish about myself. I don't even think I want to share my life with anyone now.

"There was a client of my husband with whom I became very friendly. I thought the relationship could really develop into something. We had a history. We had things in common. Interesting, but I found myself putting up all kinds of obstacles to stop the relationship. I was enjoying my independence and decided that I really didn't want to wait around for somebody else.

"My husband's death happened so fast. We had so many plans that will never be realized now. We were close, and we enjoyed being together and doing things together, and we spent a lot of time looking at what we would do with our future. That's all gone now. If it taught me anything it is that I no longer waste time with things or people I don't want in my life. Now I concentrate on surrounding myself with the things and the people I love. I don't put things off for tomorrow. I do things now. I live in this moment."

NEW BEGINNINGS

These are wonderful stories. I never get tired of hearing about the widows who have gathered the courage to move out into the world again and create a new identity for themselves. Sometimes an economic situation or dependent children don't seem to give us a choice. But whether you have money or not, I don't think that anyone can afford to retreat, to close off forever, when the world holds so many possibilities and opportunities. The not-so-simple act of putting one foot in front of the other took these widows to places they might never have gone as a partner in a marriage. Widowhood is a lousy way to learn that, and I don't recommend it to anyone, but I hope you will find comfort and hope in what these generous widows have to say. From them and in your own lives you should realize that becoming a widow can be a real release. Yes it can. It's a terrible thing, but also a tremendous turning point. A friend of mine who has been a widow for ten years put it this way:

For the first time in my life I feel strong enough to stand on my own. I've done things I'd never had done before. I'd rather he were alive. I'd rather have him back and be his wife again. But there's no denying that his death forced me to change, and for the better. It forced me to go out into the world and be independent. Other than accepting his death, it was the most difficult thing I ever faced, and I faced it alone. I'm OK now. I'd even venture to say that I'm happy.

13

RESOURCES—
WHERE TO GET HELP

Dear Lynn,

I am thirty-five years old with two children, five and seven. My husband died of a heart attack three months ago. It came as a complete shock to me. I couldn't understand it, and nobody could console me. I never thought such a thing could happen. I guess I'm like everyone else. We all think it can't happen to us. I loved my husband very much, and I know I'll never find another man like him. Besides dealing with the pain, I have money problems to worry about. Dick and I were childhood sweethearts. We always dreamed about having a life together. We married young—in fact we eloped—and my family was opposed. I didn't care what they thought. My husband worked hard for us, but we never planned ahead. We did have some insurance, but not much and some savings, and it's all going fast. I guess I lived in a dream world. Now I'm wondering what I'll do when the money's all gone. I'll have to go back to work to support us. A neighbor of mine owns a drugstore, and I'm going to ask him to give me a job. I'd really like to learn to run a computer. I'm going to have to ask my mother to help with the children, but I don't know if she will. We don't get along very well. I'd rather be home with my kids myself, but there's no hope of that. I can't believe this has happened to me—all my hopes, all my plans, right down the tubes.

There are approximately twelve million widows in the United States right now. Within the next decade, the number of widows is expected to grow beyond fifteen million. So when I say that you're not alone in the difficulties you face, I'm not kidding. Think about what those numbers could accomplish if widows united in a common cause to change some of the laws that affect our social and economic security. Suppose twelve million widows marched on Washington, D.C., to demand their rights as homemakers, as *displaced* homemakers, as the wives of veterans, as taxpayers, as voters? What a sight it would be! Maybe one day it will happen. But for today, the problem is that when it's *you* who must face the lawyer, or banker, or landlord, or Social Security office, or insurance company, you sure do feel alone. Who can you turn to for help with the many financial and legal problems you have to deal with? What can one person do when the benefit checks don't arrive, when there's a tax problem, when you have to get a job after years of working inside the home, when you need information on what free assistance programs are available, or when you need to hire someone to sort through your financial situation? What can one person do? Plenty, and I'm going to show you how.

IT CAN'T HAPPEN TO ME, EITHER

The first time I met Martin, we stayed up all night telling each other our life stories. He told me about some of his war experiences and how he won his Silver Star. He had returned home from World War II with shrapnel in his head and leg and spent three years in a veterans' hospital in West Virginia. For his injuries he was awarded a 90 percent disability pension, which at that time amounted to a little over three hundred dollars a month. The money was to be paid for life. *Martin's* life, that is. As far as I knew, through the little checking I did after we were married, the disability pension made him ineligible for commercial life insurance. I didn't know anything about insurance and I didn't want to know. What did it matter? Martin made good money as a lawyer specializing in bankruptcy (how ironic for his near-bankrupt widow), and that three hundred dollars was just icing on the cake each month. After he died, the checks stopped—immediately. But the bills kept coming, and coming, and coming.

Encouraged by friends, I kept after the Veterans Administration, but because Martin's illness wasn't service related, it said it couldn't do anything for me. It seemed to me that Martin's cancer could very well have been related in some way to his injuries, but what I thought didn't enter into the decision. At various times thereafter I wrote letters to other people, but with no luck. Someone in a New York senator's office told me that the only way the army pension could be reinstated was by a special act of Congress. They declined to follow the situation any further, and I didn't know where to go from there. Finally, I gave up.

If only I knew then what I know now. If only some of the assistance organizations that are around today existed then. I look back at that experience and know one very important fact. The Lynn Caine of today would *not* give up. I might not have gotten anything anyway, but I wouldn't have rested until I had investigated every possible avenue and knocked on every damn door I could find.

In financial and legal matters, I was a classic child bride. I was always afraid to look into our finances. Now, too late, I realize how foolish I was. I'm embarrassed to admit that when my husband died I couldn't find the will, the deed to the house, even the name of the insurance company. My sister helped me turn the house upside down before we found all the stuff I needed.

GETTING ORGANIZED

I used to refer to my office at home as the Bermuda Triangle because of the many things that disappeared in there. I think I fought being organized, and no doubt it had a lot to do with not wanting to be responsible for so many of the things that became part of my life when Martin died. I was very organized in my job as publicity director for a New York publishing company, but I had had many years to learn how to do it. Dealing with the Veterans Administration and the Social Security office was something I had to learn literally overnight, and at times I felt like I was standing in quicksand.

If Martin and I had planned ahead, so many crises could have been avoided. Out of that lack of planning came a subject I have written about and talked about since my book *Widow* was first published—Contingency Day. It's just common sense that two adults, especially those with children, would sit down at least once, and preferably once each year, and review their financial status. On Contingency Day, they would discuss steps to be taken if either husband or wife should die. As a widow, you know what a secure feeling it would have given you to immediately know what debts are outstanding, what your assets are—including stocks, bonds, certificates of deposit, real estate, and bank accounts—what your life-insurance policy means in dollars and cents, and what you're entitled to from a pension plan, social security, and other government benefits. And, most important, you would have a will, a blueprint of exactly how property is to be distributed. If you had all of those things, you would probably also have the name of a lawyer, and possibly even an accountant, to go to. In short, you wouldn't have to face what you may now face.

If you never did so before, you will now have to pull together the many documents you'll need in order to apply for, receive, or follow up on what is due to you. I'm providing you with a guideline which I call the Widow's Survival Checklist. Not everything on the list may apply to you, but gather those things that do. Before filing for benefits or conducting legal or financial transactions, ask exactly what papers you will need to accomplish a particular task. And keep copies of any new documents or agreements that come up now. It will save you a lot of time and frustration.

310

WIDOW'S SURVIVAL CHECKLIST

- The death certificate. This is a document you will need multiple original copies of, and you may not be able to use a machine copy. You can purchase additional copies, for a minimal charge, from the funeral home or from your County Health Department.

- The Social Security numbers of your family—you, your husband, and your children. If you can't find your husband's number, it should be listed on the death certificate.

- Copies of birth certificates of your family—you, your husband, and your children. If you don't have a certificate, it can be obtained from either the State or County Public Health office where the birth took place.

- Your marriage license. If you can't locate it, you can request a copy from the Office of the County Clerk where the license was issued.

- If your husband was a veteran, a certificate of honorable discharge (or other discharge). If you don't have it, many military records are kept at the Department of Defense, National Personnel Record Center, 9700 Page Blvd., St. Louis, Missouri 63132. Call this office or your local Veterans Administration for the proper request form and the address to send it to. The Department of Defense will require a copy of the death certificate in order to release any service records.

- The will. If it isn't in the house, check with your family lawyer, who should have a copy, or look in your safe-deposit box or among your husband's personal papers. If you don't have one and your property isn't registered jointly, state law will control the distribution of your assets.

- Life-insurance policy.

- Mortgage insurance or loan insurance policies.

- Accident insurance policy. This may be

separate from a general life-insurance policy.

- Auto insurance and registration numbers.

- Credit-card insurance and all credit-card numbers, outstanding balances, and credit lines.

- Records of any other debts, including the mortgage on your home and any outstanding loans.

- Employee insurance policy. Your husband may have been included under life, health, or accident insurance, and if his death was work related, there may be Workmen's Compensation coming to you.

- List of all your husband's past employers. You may be entitled to payments from more than one source.

- Union or professional organization papers. If your husband belonged to any organizations, you may be entitled to an additional source of income.

- Tax-related documents. You or your lawyer will have to contact the Internal Revenue Service (IRS). Federal estate tax will have to be filed. Unless you request an extension, your husband's federal and state income-tax forms will have to be filed at the usual time. Your local IRS office can provide you with an information booklet it issues, *Information for Survivors, Executors and Administrators*. It may be helpful.

- Records of bank accounts, stocks, bonds, safe-deposit boxes, and any investments.

For me to outline the actual, or even approximate, benefits you may be entitled to would be impossible. Benefits vary from state to state and depend largely on what kind of coverage you and your husband provided for and very often on the cause of death. What you receive from the federal agencies like the Veterans Administration and Social Security also varies. It's wise to have a lawyer, accountant, or financial adviser look through your papers once you have them together.

If your present finances don't allow for

hiring a professional, there is free assistance available, and I'll give you some leads on where to go for it. To get the ball rolling and find out what you can do about benefits, you may have to handle some of the initial leg-work yourself. That means calling each and every source of possible income and every organization, club, employer, to notify them of the death. In some cases, it may be necessary to do this in writing. You'll have to ask if you're entitled to death benefits, request information on the correct procedure you must follow to apply, and find out if there is a deadline for filing. It seems like a huge task, but no one will disagree that it's extremely important. Believe me, these people aren't going to come knocking on your door offering you bags of money. You have to go to them.

I helped to start a widows' group in our town. We have monthly meetings to inform us on how to cope with our many problems, such as banking, selling a home, taxes, stocks, fixing a car, or what have you. The widows decide what is needed and then every one hunts for a speaker. It gives all of us important information on how to handle things.

FINDING PROFESSIONAL HELP

Friends and family members can help with referrals, but if nothing pans out or that kind of information isn't available from them, there are other ways to do it.

Obviously, who you need depends on what you need. If there are legal questions involving the will, probate, property-ownership transferral, etc., you'll be looking for a lawyer. If there are financial issues, you may want an accountant or tax person, although very often a lawyer can handle all of these questions. For taxes, there are the large-volume walk-in tax services, which can effectively advise if the matter is not too complex. If you're involved with the purchase or sale of property, you may need a real estate broker; you can put together a possible list of brokers using your local Yellow Pages, or check with residents in your area. Most of these people belong to professional organizations or are licensed by some governing association, such as the American Bar Association (for lawyers), and they offer referral services of their own. Ask if a person or company is a member of a professional organization or if they hold a license to conduct business. You can use that information to find other referrals if it becomes necessary.

Many paid professionals will consent to a free-of-charge consultation as long as they know you're not just expecting free advice, or you can hire someone for an hour of consultation time. When you call to make an appointment for either of these preliminary meetings, be sure to ask what papers you need to bring with you. If you've completed your Widow's Survival Checklist, you will be prepared to discuss your situation. At the consultation meeting, you should find out what the professional can do for you, how long it will take, and how much it will cost you. Also ask when you have to pay the fee. Be absolutely sure that any agreement, including the estimate of cost to you, is made in writing. Keep a copy of it in a safe place.

Upon informing his employer that he had cancer, my husband was fired on the spot. He died eight months later. We lost our home, car, and income from his job, life, and health insurance. I ended up with a huge debt. I didn't know how to stop it from happening and don't know what to do now.

FINDING FREE ASSISTANCE

If you need professional guidance, but can't afford it, there are several free-assistance options. One of the best but often overlooked sources of information about free services is right in the front of your local telephone book. Most telephone companies provide a couple of pages of community services, which includes things like legal aid societies and senior citizens' organizations. Just because you're not sixty-five years-old doesn't mean you can't call upon a senior citizens' group for referrals. They're well-informed about what's available. You can also find everything from the Veterans Administration to the Social Security office under community services. If what you're looking for isn't listed in the directory you have, call your telephone company and find out if a special directory is available.

Another excellent source of information is your public library. It usually has all kinds of reference books—such as the *Encyclopedia of U.S. Government Benefits* and the *Government Assistance Almanac*—that can give you some good leads. Don't be afraid to ask your librarian for help. If your library is small and doesn't have a full reference shelf, call a library in the nearest large city.

For taxes, you can call the IRS for a referral to one of the programs they fund for tax counseling, such as Tax Counselling for the Elderly or the Volunteer Income Tax Assistance program (VITA).

A local college or university can be a good source of information. Just call the general number of the school and ask for a specific department, such as the legal or accounting department. They may be able to refer you to a free counseling service. Some law schools even have legal community services available to local residents.

There are many women's organizations around the country that are set up for referrals. If there's no local listing in the directory, try the nearest large city or ask your telephone company how you can find a national office. Your library may have a copy of the *Encyclopedia of Associations* (published by Gale Research, Detroit) which is a massive, nationwide listing. There are organizations like the National Organization for Women (NOW) and the League of Women Voters, which both have national offices in Washington, D.C., as well as the Society of Military Widows/National Association for

Uniformed Services, an organization based in Springfield, Virginia. Regarding veteran's benefits, you can call the Retirement Services office and the Judge Advocate General's office at the nearest military base, or try the Health Benefits Adviser at your local military medical facility.

The key to getting what you need is to be persistent. If one person can't help, ask if he or she will suggest someone who can. It requires that you take on the role of amateur sleuth, but you'll be amazed how one source will lead you to another and another until you find the help you need.

I live in a small town, and while we don't have any formal widows' group, some of us get together once a week for coffee. All of us have at one time or another felt taken by some bank, lawyer, whatever. No one seems to know what to do about it. Are we supposed to just take it?

YELLING "HELP"

One of the most common complaints I hear from widows is how they feel that people take advantage of them, and that includes paid professionals. You don't have to put up with ineffective services. When you have a complaint, speak up. If you feel some wrong has been done and the person you're dealing with isn't being reasonable, don't just sit there and take it. If the situation isn't rectified quickly, once you've made your complaint known, take the next step.

When I worked in publishing, running a large and extremely important publicity department, and anyone called me to complain about someone or something, I investigated it—and right away. My own job and professional reputation depended on my department running efficiently. The same principle applies here. If you're dealing with a lawyer who isn't doing his job, go over his head. Call his boss or senior partner, but call someone. You can always contact the American Bar Association in Chicago to file a formal complaint. If you have a problem with a tax preparer, contact the Internal Revenue Service and tell someone there about it. If the problem is with a certified public accountant, contact a State Board of Certified Public Accountants. If you have a complaint about a real estate agent, file a complaint with your State Licensing Bureau. If your insurance carrier is the culprit, you can contact your State Insurance Board. Then, too, there is always the Better Business Bureau and small-claims court, for which you don't need a lawyer. If nothing seems to work, there is still another step you can take.

YOU CAN FIGHT CITY HALL

Resolving some problems doesn't seem as clear cut as simply calling someone's boss. I remember hearing about a widow whose social security checks just stopped coming one day. She hadn't received a check in over six months and didn't know what to do about it. She had called the local office, but didn't get any results, and frankly, she was afraid to do much more about it. Finally, her niece found out about the problem and called the local office of the League of Women Voters. The representative she spoke to advised her to call the district office of Social Security, and if she didn't receive immediate results, she should call her senator's office to get some action. The woman phoned back the next day to thank the representative and say that the situation had been taken care of and the checks reinstated, but it had required a call to her senator to put the heat on. It was a simple clerical error, and within twenty-four hours it was fixed. All the fear and waiting and insecurity that widow went through before speaking up had cost her six months of worry and deprivation. It was so unnecessary, and it doesn't ever have to happen to you.

That brings to mind another widow I met recently whose landlord had received approval from the city to raise the rents in the building. Her finances were already stretched, and she had three young children to support on a limited income. She called the landlord to ask if an exception could be made, but the answer was no. Not satisfied—and aware that those few extra dollars would make more of a difference in her pocket than in her landlord's—she picked up the phone and called her senator's office. Exactly one week later she received a notice from the landlord saying that she was exempt from the rent increase. Fixed. Simple.

I told that story to a friend of mine who thought the results were terrific. But she was a little embarrassed to say that she didn't know the names of her senator or congressmen and she had no idea how a person would find out. "I never thought of that as a way to get action," she said, "but how do you actually *do* it? I mean, can you just call them up?" Yes, you can.

I am a forty-one-year-old widow with children, and I had serious financial problems. My husband was a postal employee and the Civil Service Commission took over six months to settle the claim. I feel like a victim of the system.

It's important for you to know that elected officials at local, state, and federal levels are there because you put them in office. If they don't work for you, whom do they work for? Keep that thought in mind. When you've exhausted other avenues of assistance I've given and you don't feel you're getting anywhere, ask your elected officials to intervene on your behalf. In order to get the most effective results, you need to approach them in the right way. Don't be frightened. Don't be intimidated. You are entitled to ask for their help, and usually they're willing and able to give it. They're not miracle workers and may not be able to solve all your problems, but they are equipped to cut through red tape in a way that no one else can.

The following guidelines may be useful when dealing with just about any person or organization you need to contact. I'm emphasizing elected officials because they're probably one of the least-known ways of getting attention and assistance, but you can apply these techniques in all sorts of ways. If you're dealing with an insurance company, Social Security, or your lawyer, the same basic recommendations apply. It's all a matter of clear, direct, and proper communication.

WHO'S WHO

The elected officials in your state may not live around the corner from you, but they aren't hard to find. Many have offices in Washington, D.C., and in their home state as well, and they work out of both locations. You can use either address when you want to be in touch with them. For the sake of simplicity, I'm using Washington, D.C.

I've already mentioned two very underrated resources, the telephone book and the library, and both can provide you with the information you need here as well. At the back of many telephone directories, there's a separate section (sometimes referred to as the "blue pages") where you'll find listings for all kinds of public and government agencies—everything from day care to the Housing Authority. They also list the names, addresses, and telephone numbers of senators, congressmen, and other elected officials. If you call the library, it will no doubt have a copy of the *Congressional Directory*, which is published by the Superintendent of Documents (Washington, D.C.), and the *United States Government Manual*. Either of these may be helpful for finding the right person or place for you to contact with a problem. You can also call your local office of the League of Women Voters.

I had numerous notices, month after month, from the Social Security Administration that I was receiving duplicate payments for my child and would be prosecuted. I was not receiving any payments, let alone duplicates. My friendly neighborhood congressman finally got that mess straightened out.

LETTER WRITING

The letters that representatives and senators receive are their main connection to their constituents, and the politician who doesn't listen to what's going on back home may not be in office for long. They all get bushels of mail every day, and it *is* read and answered, if not personally, then by a staff member. Letter writing is an effective way for you to communicate a problem, and it's simple and cheap. The reply you receive may refer you elsewhere to another government agency or official, or it may offer a solution. But you will know that you've been heard.

Now that you know where to write to, let's concentrate on some of the basics. Use the proper form when you're addressing a public official. Your salutation should be as follows:

FOR FEDERAL OFFICIALS

U.S.	U.S.
SENATOR	**REPRESENTATIVE**
Honorable J. Doe	Honorable J. Doe
United States Senate	House of Representatives
Washington, D.C. 20510	Washington, D.C. 20515
Dear Senator Doe,	Dear Congressman/
	Congresswoman Doe,

FOR STATE OFFICIALS

GOVERNOR
Honorable J. Doe
Governor of———————
Executive Chambers
City, State (zip code)

Dear Governor Doe,

STATE SENATOR
Honorable J. Doe
———————State Senate
City, State (zip code)

Dear Senator Doe,

FOR CITY OFFICIALS

MAYOR

Honorable J. Doe
Mayor of the City
 of———
City Hall
City, State (zip code)

Dear Mayor Doe,

**PRESIDENT OF
THE CITY
COUNCIL**
Honorable J. Doe
President of the City
 Council
City Hall
City, State (zip code)

Dear President Doe,

CITY COUNCIL MEMBER	DISTRICT ATTORNEY
Honorable J. Doe	Honorable J. Doe
City Council,	District Attorney
City Hall	of———
City, State (zip code)	City, State (zip code)
Dear Councilman/ Councilwoman Doe,	Dear District Attorney Doe,

Here are some hints about what you should say and the best way to say it:

Do

- You should use the proper salutation I've given above.

- Make sure that you spell the person's name correctly.

- Be absolutely sure to include your return address. You'd be surprised how many people don't and are furious that they never get a reply. I know it's very common because a lot of people forget it in the letters they write to me, too.

- It's OK to write a letter in longhand, rather than with a typewriter, but be sure it's legible. You won't get an answer if no one can read it.

- Be as courteous as you can. That may not be easy if you're at a point where you feel no one is listening or cares, but remember that you're asking for help.

- Keep a copy of your letter in case there is a need to follow up. It does happen that things get lost, and if you have to write again you should be able to give the addressee a copy of the first letter.

Don't

- There's no point in threatening anyone or apologizing for taking up their time. Threats aren't likely to get you what you want, and apologies just take up valuable space in your letter.

- Don't ramble on for ten pages giving your life story. No one will have the time to read your letter. Try to limit yourself to a page or two and give the necessary details and background and state your problem clearly.

- Don't leave out important information like a social security number or a copy of military discharge papers, if necessary. Enclose machine copies of papers, not originals.

A MORE PERSONAL APPROACH

Sometimes a situation is really an emergency, as in the case of the widow who stopped receiving her social security checks for six months. In such a case, there may not be time to write a letter and wait for a reply. There's nothing wrong with picking up the telephone. It's unlikely that you'll be able to speak directly to a senator, mayor, or congressman, but you will reach someone who works for them. It's the job of their staff to field calls and be informed in ways that help voters. Frequently, they're even more informed than the people they work for. Make a list of what you want to say before you make your call. It will help you to be clear about what you need and make it much easier for the person on the other end of the telephone to give you an answer.

My husband and I used to periodically review our finances. All the papers would come out and be spread over the dining room table. We would sit together and bring everything up to date. Now that I'm a widow, I'm glad we handled things the way we did. I encourage my friends to do the same but am shocked at how they believe it can never happen to them.

REPLANNING FOR THE FUTURE

If you and your husband never held a Contingency Day, it is time for you to hold one for yourself. While you're reviewing benefits to which you're entitled now, you should also be planning for the future, and that includes writing a new will and possibly arranging guardianship for your children. If you've been left without the benefit of proper coverage after your husband's death, don't allow the same thing to happen to your dependents if something should happen to you. One of the most important things to get in order first is your own life and medical insurance, and there is some good news about that.

A federal law (PL 99-272) was enacted in 1986 that offers temporary continuation of group coverage for widows (also divorced or separated spouses) and their children from your husband's employer if you were originally included in his plan. You have to pay both the amount that was deducted from your husband's paycheck for insurance and the amount that the employer put in, plus a small fee (3 percent of the premium), but it will give you full coverage for eighteen to thirty-six months after his death. It's a lot less expensive than commercial insurance, and you don't have to take a physical exam to qualify. In most cases, the extension applies only to businesses that employ twenty or more people and to state and local government health plans. You should check with the employer, the insurance carrier, or your lawyer for details.

If the above coverage isn't available to you, there are other solutions:

- There are a number of membership organizations that offer insurance programs. Being part of one of these group insurance approaches makes it cheaper for everyone. You can try the following:

American Association of Retired Persons
(AARP)
1909 K St., NW
Washington, D.C. 20049
(202) 872-4700

The National Council of Jewish Women
15 E. Twenty-sixth St.
New York, N.Y. 10010
(212) 532-1740

Co-op America
2100 M St., NW, #310
Washington, D.C. 20063
(202) 872-5307

• Health maintenance organizations (HMO's) offer a wide range of health services for a monthly payment, and they're usually less expensive than the commercial varieties. Often the choice of physicians is restricted. To find these organizations, call your American Medical Association in Chicago to find your state medical association, or look in the Yellow Pages of the telephone book. Shop around to find where you can get the best coverage for the money.

- If you're over sixty-five or disabled, contact your local Social Security office for Medicare or Medicaid information.

- If you have a job, you should be entitled to your own employer group coverage, and you can include your children under the plan.

- There is, of course, always commercial insurance, but it can be expensive. You can find the names of many insurance companies in your Yellow Pages. Shop around for the best deal.

I'm forty-six years old and have been widowed for just over a year. I need to go back to work because I don't have enough money to live on. I haven't worked in many years and wonder if it's too late for me to start again.

After you have done all the things you can do to receive the benefits you're entitled to, there sometimes remains the problem of not having enough insurance or savings or other income to cover your needs. This brings up the questions of returning to work. Considering that the average age of widows in this country is fifty-six and a large percentage of them have been out of the work force for many years or have never worked outside the home, the prospect of finding a job may not seem very bright. I can't paint a rosy picture of the employment scene for you. The truth, according to *The State-by-State Guide to Women's Legal Rights* (by The N.O.W./Legal Defense and Education Fund and Dr. Renee Cherow-O'Leary, McGraw-Hill, 1987), is that a third of all widows live below the poverty level, and less than 10 percent receive pension survivor benefits. Most of these women are trying to venture into the job markets when they are between the ages of fifty and fifty-nine. They're beginning their employment close to retirement age, and as a result most wind up in low-paying, dead-end jobs. Whether you're twenty-six or fifty-six, there's no question that it's tough to reenter the work scene, but there are various resources available that can help get you started. If your financial situation is desperate, you may have to take a lesser job while looking and planning for something better. Paying the most urgent bills and keeping food on the table are your priorities.

The job I had was not what I'd call a dead end, but it sure paid a miserably low salary, as many publishing positions do. I had two young children to support and had to learn to stretch the money in ways I had never imagined before. But I plunged ahead and did the best I could. The job was good for me. I was busy all the time, and the work demanded a great deal from me. It also gave me the opportunity to meet people, and that was something I also badly needed. The publication of *Widow* put me in the public spotlight, and eventually I left my job in publishing to devote myself full time to seminars and lectures and my books. That, too, has been extremely demanding, and the financial rewards are not nearly as great as you might think. If I look back at what I've done to support myself and my family, I can see that the reason I was able to do as well as I did is that I wouldn't allow myself to be afraid to take risks. I think that a willingness to work hard, to learn, and to somehow call up a bit of bravery you might not think you have can carry you a long way. If you need a job, no matter what your age or what situation you're in, it is time now to pull yourself up straight and walk boldly out the front door. I can't and won't pretend that it's easy, but with perseverance and faith in yourself you can do many surprising things.

I worked for a newspaper nearly twenty years ago, but quit when we decided to have a family. To my mind, I've still had a job these last twenty years. What do people think I've been doing, sitting on my ass? But that kind of work experience doesn't qualify me to do anything.

DISPLACED HOMEMAKERS PLEASE APPLY

The term "displaced homemaker" was coined in 1974 by the late Tish Sommers, a cofounder of the Older Women's League. Until then, there wasn't any term to describe the millions of women "whose primary occupation has been in the home and who are left with few resources by divorce, separation, the death or disability of a spouse, or by the loss of public assistance" (Displaced Homemakers Network). That description may not mean much from where you're sitting now, but it does finally designate a "group" that requires assistance, and it has sparked some activity among lawmakers. Some of the following resources for job placement assistance are a direct result of that activity, and I will discuss what you can do to further the cause. But first, let's concentrate on the various ways you can find job training and job placement.

FINDING A JOB

- Let helpful friends and relatives know that you're in the market for a job. You never know where a lead may come from, so it's a good idea to announce that you're actively seeking employment. Ignore those negative people who think you're too inexperienced or too old or too whatever. I know of a woman who at sixty-one took a position as a part-time secretary and did fine. She even learned how to use a word processor.

- Contact the board of education in your area and find out if it offers courses in job training. They're usually very inexpensive. If you can't pay for it, ask if financial assistance is available.

- Call a local college. Many schools offer

job counseling or have programs available for women seeking employment.

- The United States Employment Service works with state employment agencies to provide free counseling and job placement. It maintains job banks that list vacancies in each particular region of the country and offers referral services for training programs. Check your phone book under state government listings for your state employment agency. It should be listed in the community services section I mentioned earlier.

- Under the Job Training Partnership Act (JTPA), the federal government finds training programs. They're coordinated through your local elected officials and private industry councils designated by the governor of each state. Contact your state department of labor for information.

- Check with the local Young Women's Christian Association (YWCA). Many have training courses or job counseling available for women.

- Contact the Displaced Homemakers Network. It offers a countrywide referral service through which you can find help in locating job training, putting together a résumé, and finding a job. A terrific resource.

- If you have some idea of what you can offer an employer, there are plenty of privately run employment agencies. Before they do anything for you, make sure that you are not responsible for paying a fee for any service.

Is there any way in which we widows can unite our efforts so that we will be heard when gross inequities exist in our laws? As one lone widow, I have no chance of being heard in Washington. There are probably others who have this same problem.

There are many things you can do and places you can contact for all kinds of assistance and problem solving, but there is still much to be done for widows. A friend of mine used to refer to widows as the "invisible legion." She said, "For all that we contribute to life in this country, from child rearing to running for public office and everything in between, widows still get the short end of the stick in too many cases. The way widows continue to be treated is a disgrace, and someone should do something about it." I used to ask her who she thought should be doing the doing, and she'd say, "How the hell do I know? I'm only one person."

You are not just one person. You're a member of a large community of widows that is twelve million strong and growing. A group like that can move mountains and lawmakers and an entire country to change their way of thinking. I have had that same conversation with many other widows and can now offer a way for "just one person" to join in and really be an effective force toward making necessary changes.

The loudest voice you have should be used on Election Day. But before you cast a vote, find out where a candidate for office stands on the issues that affect you. Write letters, read newspapers, pick up the phone. Ask questions like "Where do you stand on the Equal Rights Amendment [ERA]?" Do you know that the ERA was first introduced in Congress in 1923, and it still hasn't passed? The time for it will come again, and you can help make it happen. Ask questions like

"Where do you stand on widows' rights to veterans' benefits, counseling and training programs for displaced homemakers, and reduced rates for life and health insurance for widows?" Whatever concerns you concerns other widows, and you *can* do something about it. I want to close this chapter with a listing of some of the organizations you can contact to lend your voice or services or whatever you feel you want to contribute to improving the lives of all widows. You can call on them for help, referrals, information, too—but it works both ways.

Displaced Homemakers
  Network
1411 K St., NW,
Suite 930
Washingon, D.C.
20005

National Organization
for Women
1401 New York Ave.,
NW, Suite 800
Washington, D.C.
20005-2102

Gray Panthers
311 S. Juniper St.,
Suite 601
Philadelphia, Pa. 19107

Older Women's
League (OWL)
730 Eleventh St.,
NW, Suite 300
Washington, D.C.
20001

The League of Women
  Voters
1730 M St., NW
Washington, D.C. 20036

National Council of
  Senior Citizens
925 Fifteenth St., NW
Washington, D.C. 20005

Widowed Persons
  Service
American Association
  of Retired Persons
1909 K St., NW
Washington, D.C.
20049

YWCA of the USA
726 Broadway
New York, N.Y.
10003

14

FOR THOSE WHO CARE

Dear Mrs. Caine,

As a student who will be graduating in three months from the California State University and due to my intent to build my occupation and profession around working with the dying and bereaved, I felt I had to write to you. I heard you speak in Los Angeles, and you and your story really made an impression on me. Death indeed is still in many ways ostracized from our society's consciousness. Too many people are still uncomfortable talking about death. I plan to become a professional who learns to help in an honest way those who need to understand themselves and accept death.

I feel that I have something special to offer in that my mother is a widow. When my father died five years ago, I tried to understand as best I could what my mother was going through, but I didn't. She would occasionally speak to me about it, about her inability to cry, about her fears, etc. Only recently have I begun to empty my head of intellectualizations and work to understand the pain I know my mother lived with for so long and which she will probably remember for the rest of her life. Mrs. Caine, in writing to you I have been extremely impulsive, with no plan or idea of exactly what I need to say. I think I have a better idea of what I want to do with my life, and I want to say thank you.

Receiving letters like the one that opens this chapter is very gratifying to me. The audience I have always tried to reach has been the widow herself, because I felt that was where help was needed most. But my personal story seems to have spilled over into a parallel audience that includes many people who are in one way or another in contact with widows. It's been a happy surprise for me to get the positive feedback this letter gives, and over the years I've received quite a few of them. Comments and calls and letters and discussions have come from a wide range of people who are the children, parents, or friends of widows. I've also received feedback from professionals: doctors, lawyers, insurance agents, clergy, students and teachers, even funeral directors. There are so many people who really want to help that I felt it was time to talk about the needs of widows from a different perspective. I want to speak to those who care about what the widow feels, what she faces, and what you can do to help her.

As a friend or family member who is grieving for a loved one, you may be feeling the added pressure of wanting to ease another person's pain and not knowing how to do it. If you're a professional person, the widow may come to you for guidance or assistance on matters she has never before had to deal with. She may seem frightened, withdrawn, and unable to cope. And if you don't understand the behavior patterns of grief, you may be uncertain about the best way to proceed.

The need for patience by those who are around widows is tremendous. I don't think many people understand that.

Martin's death affected my life in so many ways. I was left nearly bankrupt and with two young children to raise. I had a job that

347

didn't pay much, and it required my attention, enthusiasm, and energy every day. I was grateful to be working, but the demands were such that I couldn't afford "off days." I also had to deal with my grief and the emotional turmoil that came with it. For a long time, my pain was intense, and I constantly walked a tightrope between pretending I was fine and being honest about the fact that I wasn't. I put on a courageous face to the world, but I was a mess underneath. Some of my friends sensed my stress, and a few witnessed the way in which it manifested itself. I retreated entirely, or I was depressed and at times very angry, dependent, needy, and certainly frightened and confused. Most of them didn't know what to do to help me. They didn't know what to say, how to comfort me, how to make it better, and at the time I was in no position to tell them.

Professional people have a somewhat different place in the life of a widow. They don't necessarily have a personal connection to her, and their main concern is to do a job—whether it's legal, financial, whatever—and just get on with it. Why should they want to get involved anyway? Grief isn't attractive or easy or profitable, and who has the time to bother? Most don't. But I'll tell you this, I've had the privilege of coming in contact with some terrific professional people who did their job, but whose warmth and sensitivity really made a difference in my life. I like to think they aren't the exceptions.

Although we're better educated about death and bereavement today, most people, professional or not, continue to be uncomfortable being around a grieving widow. I hope the information in this chapter will help to change that. It crosses the boundaries of professional and personal relationships with the widow. I haven't separated the two because the basics remain the same for everyone.

I want you to know that your willingness to assist in the healing process can do a lot of good. Obviously, the first step is to be interested in the woman who is grieving, to care. Since this book has landed in your hands, perhaps that first step has already been taken.

It's strange how people recognize the obvious miseries of life like alcoholism, drug addiction, blindness, etc., and I'm certainly not making light of them, but the simple loss of love and the loneliness that goes with it are the accepted imperfections of life.

THE LOOK OF GRIEF

Sometime in the late seventies, I was interviewed for a film made by the Pentera Group, Inc. The film focused on some of the financial problems I faced after Martin died and is still used as a training tool for insurance companies. I talked about the role insurance people play in helping couples plan for a time when the husband or wife might die, and I spoke mainly about the more practical aspects of widowhood, like wills, insurance, and guardianship. I recently saw the film again and was pleased to hear myself include among the financial facts of life and death a message to the audience advising them to educate themselves about widowhood, and I meant it not just from the standpoint of selling insurance. I stressed the importance of caring and of personal conviction and suggested that they make an effort to understand human psychology. While watching that film, a thought occurred that I think is the foundation of this chapter. It is simply that a widow feels pain, but not the kind of pain most people are familiar with. If your client or friend or sister were a woman with two broken legs in casts, you would visibly see that she was dealing with a problem. The wounds of widowhood are not so easily seen with the eyes because the process of grief is experienced beneath the skin, within the heart, and somewhere deep in the soul. But, believe me, the pain of grief is severe. The fact that it's an internal process can mean that you receive and respond to mixed signals and you can misread what's going on with the widow. As I've said, I was outwardly a pillar of strength, capable and strong. I went to my job each day and did what was expected of me. I returned home each evening and fell apart. The truth is that on most days I was really shaky, vulnerable, lacking self-confidence, and terrified. If you are aware that what you see may very well not represent what's really happening with that internal process, you will begin to understand the need for sensitivity and compassion on your part. That means that your actions and efforts on behalf of the widow should not be guided only by what you see, but by the knowledge that there's a great deal more than that to grief.

My brother and I were appalled—shocked would be a better term—at how our mother regressed before our eyes as the months went by after our father's death. I was enraged at how she "let me down." I thought that her "predeath" days, in which she was mature, strong, and rational with a great ability to cope were made phony by her dissolution into self-pity and childish tirades.

HOW LONG DOES GRIEF LAST?

If there is one characteristic of grief that you should know about, it's that there's no blueprint for it. There is no road map to tell you that yesterday the woman who is widowed was at point A and next week she'll be at point C. Grief doesn't work that way. I know how much more difficult things can be when the people around you don't understand that grief isn't conducted in an orderly and structured manner. Those who haven't experienced it themselves usually only want their friend or family member to feel better, to get on with her life. If she feels better, so will you. There isn't a simple solution to grief because it's an ongoing process. It won't be rushed or pushed. A widow who is very active in a local widows' group in New Orleans told me, "My husband died nearly twelve years ago, and I still have a very vivid memory of a friend of mine sitting me down over coffee one morning. She started to firmly tell me that I was wasting everyone's time by what she called wallowing in my misery. That was almost exactly eight months after my husband died, and I was still having a terrible time just handling the most simple tasks. I started to cry, and she started to raise her voice to me. 'Do you want everyone to think you've lost your mind?' she said. 'You have to snap out of this. We all worry about you, but frankly, we're sick and tired of seeing you behave like a child.' I was horrified, and unfortunately I believed her. I started to think something was wrong with me. The worst thing was that she thought she was doing the right thing. She didn't mean any harm. I found out later from the counseling group I joined that she was completely wrong. It took a long time for me to forgive her. Her problem was that she was watching the clock tick by and observing me week after week, and to her it must have seemed that I was making no progress at all. She just didn't understand."

There are stages to grief that include shock, numbness, denial, panic, depression, anger, and acceptance, but one stage doesn't follow another in a straight line. There is a weaving back and forth between all the stages. It's not as if the widow won't revisit earlier steps, and she may do so again and again. She may seem to be standing solidly on her own two feet, caring for her family and holding a job, when suddenly twelve months after the death it appears that she has moved backward to where she was at three months. Although the list of stages of grief I've given is accurate, no one can predict what feelings or problems will emerge at any given time. It may be frustrating for you to observe the weaving and overlapping process that seems to take a person one step forward and two back. The only answer to it is showing patience and allowing it to unfold. You can't and shouldn't try to direct it or control it. The widow will move through each of these stages in a path of her own making in order to finally reach acceptance. Every widow's timetable is different, so trying to push and shove her forward will lead nowhere and probably cause a lot of additional stress.

My father had a cancerous brain tumor

removed, and it took him nearly a year to die. It was hell. It was my mother who went through such turmoil. I never understood why she acted so strange. I criticized her, found fault in everything she did, argued, and finally started to build a brick wall between our once loving relationship.

Keep in mind the fact that more than anything else, the widow in your life needs to know that you are there to help no matter how long it takes. That's not exactly the usual reaction we have. Most people feel that the death should be forgotten as soon as possible. They're in a hurry for everything to snap back into place again. It isn't easy to allow grief to be resolved at its own pace, but that is exactly what you should do. I don't mean to say that you can't be of help by offering support or your loving presence, but you are not supposed to set yourself up as the judge of when the pain should be gone and life should once again be normal. If you remember that and put it into practice, you will be helping more than you know.

I spent long nights on the telephone with my closest friend who lived in another state. It was a while before I noticed that it was I who was doing all the talking. I had never realized how wise my friend was. She knew that I needed to talk.

LEARN TO LISTEN

Almost everyone worries about what to say to a widow. You don't want to hurt anyone's feelings or make anyone upset. But more important than knowing what to say is knowing how to listen.

One of the professional terms used to describe the widow's need to talk is "obsessive reminiscence." Widows need to ask about and to tell what they've been through. "How could things have gone so wrong? How could he have died? Was it that cough, or was it that fall?" It may seem that all the widow talks about is the death of her husband, but there's a good reason for it. The death, sudden or after a long illness, is more than she can grasp initially, and so by externalizing, by talking it out and putting it out, she can begin to see it as real. The more real it becomes, the less the obsessive need to talk about it. It is predictable and normal that widows review over and over again the way

356

the death occurred, and they should be encouraged to do so. These are not exactly socially acceptable topics of conversation. We've been trained from an early age not to bring them up in public. When someone else does, it's almost a reflex action to end the conversation or steer it away to something more cheerful. It may sound like someone is dwelling on things that are better forgotten. Believe me, no one wishes they could be forgotten more than the widow. But part of grieving and of working toward acceptance is often done by repeatedly examining, dissecting, and analyzing the event.

Hearing about pain and sorrow and death can also bring to light our own feelings of inadequacy. What if you don't say the right thing? What if you upset her more? The widow can say over and over again, "How did it happen? I can't believe it. Why did he die?" You are not expected to have the answers to these questions. It is the saying that's important, not your opinion of why or how death occurred. I value honesty, and I know that it's healthy for widows. You can say, "I don't know what to say and I don't have the answer, but I just want you to know that I will be with you during this time. You tell me what you're feeling, and

I'll listen. You tell me what I can do to help, and I'll do it if I can." Be honest, but sensitive. Often the best you can do is just to offer a warm presence and an open heart.

I always recommend that you avoid euphemisms when speaking about death. A widow told me about a man she worked with who always noticeably lowered his voice when speaking to her about "what had happened." "He made me feel so awkward," she said. "He would walk up to me and almost whisper as though we were in a spy ring and the news was top secret. Then he'd say things like, 'I'm sure it's difficult when a loved one departs.' " I'm a great believer in calling things by their right names. It speeds acceptance. Stay away from euphemisms. They are a form of denial and won't contribute to acceptance of the fact that a *death* has occurred.

Another common reaction to the widow's need to talk about death is that the discomfort we feel from it can be so overwhelming that we tend to distance ourselves, even run away. I think it makes us realize how out of control we are, or maybe our discomfort arises from a fear of being out of control. If this death happened, other deaths can happen. That thought leads us to confront our own vulnerability and the truth that no one is exempt from death. I remember an interesting and probably positive result among some of my women friends who witnessed my grief and who felt that vulnerability in their own lives. I found that some of them were kinder in their relationships with their husbands or just appreciated their own lives more. Knowing the way Martin's death had changed my life gave them the understanding that their lives could just as easily be changed. If the subject of death makes you uncomfortable, I hope it will help to know that most people feel the same way. But understand that there is a real need for the widow to talk. Don't worry about being conversational. Listening is much more important. It is the medium by which the widow is able to participate in her own feelings. It's one of the ways they are resolved. It brings the widow that much closer to acceptance. I always advise widows to find an appropriate environment through a counseling service in order to be able to express themselves freely, but the support system that surrounds the widow is important, too. I've been on both sides of the fence in that I've run widows' groups myself and have done counseling work on a one-to-one basis with widows. I've also experienced the effects of counseling on my own grief. I think I have a broader perspective on the subject than most, and so I don't mind repeating how important it is to simply be a good listener.

I could just not begin to understand what my sister was going through, and because of her personality, I thought her cold and very tight. I wish I knew what was going on within. I wish I had enough insight to offer her the support she never asked anyone for (but would have liked, I think).

THE FEELINGS OF GRIEF

Frequently, with the talking and the listening come the tears and sometimes more intense displays of emotion. More than words, emotions *really* make us uncomfortable. The most common and immediate response we have to the strong emotions that come with grief is to try to squash them. "There, there, now, everything is going to be OK. Don't cry. Get a good night's sleep, and you'll feel better in the morning." Don't pretend that you know how the widow is feeling. Unless you've been there yourself, you don't. Releasing emotion is a critical part of the healing process, but I can't pretend that it's easy to be around. That's one of the reasons I recommend that widows put themselves in an environment where they feel comfortable and safe in allowing these emotions to flow. It is so important that the widow be encouraged to express her feelings that I can't stress it enough. Storing powerful emotions inside isn't healthy, physically or emotionally, and medical science supports that time and time again. It may be one of the reasons widows have such a high mortality rate, and knowing that may enable you to let her express herself as she needs to. If you are mourning the death as well, it may give you the opportunity to release difficult emotions, too. You really can't take away the tears, the anger, or the sadness and make things right anyway. If you tell her how she should feel, you are pushing that emotion down deeper, and it becomes stronger and more complicated to deal with later on. You have to allow, not control. If you are present during some emotional time and can't handle it, understand your own feelings in terms of what you can deal with and what you can't. There are times when it is advisable to recommend professional help, but don't be surprised if

361

your advice isn't taken. You may be able to tell a widow where she can go for assistance, but she is the one who must take the initiative to receive it. I have frequently put widows in touch with counseling groups. I know that some women follow up and some don't. You and I have no control over that. I would hope that if your suggestion is made with compassion and sincerity, the widow will seek the help she needs.

My friends pulled me through, preserving my sanity. Without their patience and kindness I would not have made it, I'm sure. But the callousness of people like our family lawyer shocked me.

THE WIDOW'S RESPONSE

There is one fact about widowhood that overrules all others. It is that the widow who is experiencing the loss, who is grieving, cannot erase the source of her pain. She cannot delete it from her life. That makes her different from you, and makes her feel less in charge of her own fate. She is set apart from other people because her husband is dead. It makes her angry, resentful. Other women have husbands. She doesn't. Your life goes on, but she feels that the future has been grabbed right out of her hands. That makes her extremely sensitive to the things you say or do. The widow cannot tell people how to act toward her because, for the most part, they don't listen. That's why I'm telling you.

The initial impact of death is shock and numbness, and it is a time of nonfeeling. It's only after the first few weeks or months pass and that numbness begins to lift that the floodgates of conflicting, overlapping feelings and emotions begin to surface. Anne Rosberger, a friend of mine who counsels widows, told me, "Widows can become enraged when people say thoughtless or tactless things to them. Particularly after the numb period, the widow is indeed almost skinless, as though all her nerve endings are exposed. If anyone rubs up against her in the slightest way, it hurts her terribly. She can turn and attack. People have to understand that it's not maliciousness on the part of the bereaved. It is her way of protecting herself. She feels maligned, hurt, so any additional pain or difficulties are often more than she can tolerate."

I have taught assertiveness-training courses and offer a chapter in this book for widows to learn about it. It is your task to understand why it's necessary to have assertiveness training in the first place. Since you are not the widow, you can't know what it feels like to have your world shattered and to feel that you are left alone to pick up the pieces. But by my description, I hope that you will have some insight into why your words and actions toward a widow should be chosen carefully. Many widows are so traumatized after their husbands' death that they express themselves in ways that sometimes appear irrational. Maybe it really is irrational, but death —and the feeling that someone you love has been taken from you—doesn't seem to the widow to be a very rational occurrence. I vacillated between being stoic and brave and acting like a crazy woman. I've talked about how I followed men on the street who looked like Martin. Is that rational? I've written about how I sent a letter to a politician asking for five hundred thousand dollars because he was fat and rich and I was poor and thin. Is that rational? Martin was dead, and I felt I was left with nothing. I didn't think *that* was rational. Then I would turn around and hear someone ask what I was going to do about my sex life, or why I didn't go out and buy a low-cut dress, or why I didn't give up my apartment and move to the suburbs (which I did and lived to regret). Or I would hear comments like "Hi Lynn, how is your miserable life anyway?" and "Why aren't you smiling, Lynn? You always look so serious." I tell widows as part of the assertiveness training that most people don't mean to say things that hurt, but it's usually simple thoughtlessness. I know that's true. The answer for you is to think carefully about your choice of words and the message they convey. Stop for a second before you speak and ask yourself if what you're about to say is really going to help the widow who is "skinless" to feel better.

Part of that thought process should also include staying away from giving advice. "Everyone seems to know what's best for me," widows tell me. "Everyone is an expert when it comes to my life and what I should be doing." My advice to widows is to sit tight for a time and make no major decisions. That includes moving to a new place, changing jobs, and anything that will further upset the life that is already turned inside out. If you think you know what's best for the widow, you probably don't. If you decide to help her, wait for a time and let those shattered pieces begin to come back together again. You'll be a lot closer to doing what's best for her. Friends advised me to move to New Jersey, and I did. It was a bad decision, but they meant well. Other friends advised me to date men before I was ready, and I did. It was a bad decision and caused me unhappiness, but they meant well. You, too, probably mean well, so that's all the more reason for you to take *my* advice and not offer advice. Give the widow time to get herself in order. Obviously, there may be legal questions or financial decisions to be made that cannot be put off, and I don't mean to suggest that you should sit by and allow the IRS to close off someone's bank accounts because of nonpayment of taxes. But remember that a major life change has taken place and the widow needs time to pull herself back together before any further upsetting events are dealt with.

My best friend's husband died recently. They were to many of their friends the perfect couple and were supposed to celebrate their fourth wedding anniversary a month after he died. My friend is having a rough time, and I want so much to help her.

Other comments that are frequently made to widows are "Please let us know what we can do to help"; "You must come see us for the weekend. I'm sure a change of scenery would do you good"; and 'Just let me know if you need anything." These words are practically an automatic response when someone close to you has a problem or is in trouble. How many of you have ever really followed up on this kind of offer? It's something that infuriates widows. People make a big show of concern, and then zilch happens. I tell widows that when someone offers to help, take them up on it. "Sure, can you pick up my laundry on Thursday. My car is out of commission." They usually find out very quickly who is sincere about wanting to help. Let me tell you: If you make an offer to help, mean it. Make it your business to find out what needs to be done. Make yourself available. And don't say, "If you need money, just ask." If you're serious about it, put a check in an envelope and quietly give it to the widow. She can return it if it isn't needed. Empty words and empty offers don't go unnoticed by widows.

BRINGING ORDER TO CHAOS

Have you ever been in a situation where you were so anxious that you walked away not remembering a word anyone said? Or have you ever had such a case of nerves that you couldn't recall later who was in the room with you? Many people, even in the best of times, have had this kind of reaction when they felt uncertain or a little frightened. Afterward, you feel so foolish, so stupid and inadequate. I don't think that anyone would argue that grief and widowhood are not the best of times. With the shock of death comes a disintegration of identity for many widows. The partnership of marriage is split in two, or as many widows describe it, "I feel like half a person." There may be insecurity about financial survival even if there is plenty of money. There is definitely confusion and disorientation.

A widow I did some counseling work with a few years ago told me that her husband had always handled the finances in the family. She was certainly competent to do it herself, but that was the way they set up their marriage and they were comfortable with it. Seven months after her husband died she told me, "If I saw his name on my checkbook, our checkbook, it just ripped me apart. Because here was something joint, and it's no longer joint. I could barely remember how to put food on the table for my children because I was worrying about the lousy checkbook and paying bills. I didn't care. I couldn't concentrate on anything for long. I had to learn very quickly to take over the house alone and to care for our children and make decisions about what to do about my husband's business. I didn't feel that I knew what I was doing. I was walking around in a thick fog. I was looking for someone to direct me. I wanted someone to say to me, 'If you say this or do that everything will be OK.' It was all too much for me."

Most widows experience a temporary loss of ability to concentrate on anything for very long. I always think of it as a natural protective shield that is activated when reality is too much to bear. Even reading a newspaper or magazines requires more energy than they have to give. The insecurity is intense, the lack of identity and confidence terrifying. I used to wake up during the middle of the night in a cold sweat, sure that I could become a bag lady living in the street or that I would become crippled and unable to care for my children or go to work. Even widows who are financially stable have these fears. I'm telling you all of this so that you understand that the world becomes a very confusing and unfriendly place, and often the widow's response to it is to shut down, to retreat, and to feel that she cannot cope at all. The most simple tasks grow into something monumental. I think that most people can understand this reaction, but not the fact that it can go on for a long time and reach into every minor responsibility that the widow is now in charge of. The usual reactions from people are to step in and take over or to demand that she stand on her own two feet and deal competently, when her state of mind is just about as bad as it can get. Those of you who care about the widow's welfare must walk a fine line between the two reactions. If you take command of her life, you're really not helping her to learn how to cope. If you leave her to her own devices, you're contributing to more confusion and possibly bad decision making that can have far-reaching effects on her and her family's future. I will say again that this is not a question of competency, but of an inability to focus, to concentrate, due to an overwhelming shock.

I can't teach you everything there is to know about crisis behavior in one chapter, but I can reduce to simple terms the best way to assist widows through the turmoil and confusion and the feelings of being unable to cope.

Your role is to speak to her in a way that is neither demeaning nor patronizing and at the same time to be aware that much of her concentration is not quite there. In practical terms that means no long lectures or speeches, even short ones, about the way things should be done or about how you know she can't handle anything right now so you'll do it for her. It means going over things step by step and writing the details down so that she can peruse them later. It means not expecting her to commit to memory the details of her financial status or real estate holdings or even what she plans to have for dinner, but making a list of things that need to be dealt with so they can be handled one at a time.

Shock does something to the mind that causes ambiguity and uncertainty, which produces indecisiveness and dependency. "What do you think I should do?" is a common question asked by widows. Widows don't want to take the chance that one of their decisions could create any more problems. They recoil, beg off, and don't make any decisions. They procrastinate. It's a kind of psychic paralysis that leads to thinking like "I know I should do this and this. I just can't seem to make myself do it." The antidote for that is clear guidance and firm direction. You shouldn't take over their tasks, but you can prescribe specific, clear steps that should be taken in order of their importance and priority. It just adds to the overall sense of stupidity and uselessness if you have a stack of papers in front of you and no idea where to begin. I've been in banks where I've asked about some investment and was just handed brochures written in a language I didn't understand. That isn't enough. You have to take the widow through it slowly, make notes, and be willing to go through it again. You will be allowing her to slowly regain control. You will be steering her in the direction in which she will finally be back in charge of her life.

My daughter recently came to visit me after a two-year absence. We had a falling out after her father died, and she married a man I didn't approve of. She recently came to tell me how sorry she was and how she had not realized what I was going through. She brought up the time she told me I was a nut case. She had been so used to a happy mother that she didn't understand the person I became. She has developed a deeper understanding of what happened, and we have been able to begin to capture the closeness we once enjoyed.

HOPE FOR THE FUTURE

When I became a widow, I didn't have any role model or a guide like this book. They just didn't exist then. No one talked about death or widowhood, so for the most part, I was left to my own devices. There were friends and even a few professional people who showed me I could regain my footing and carry on with my life, but I credit myself in many ways. It was I who had to get out there and try when I didn't feel like it, and it was I who finally took command of my future. But for a long time, I didn't think I had one. I'll always cherish the friend who told me not to worry that I had no money. "You are one of the most resourceful women I know," he said. "When you're ready to dig into those resources, you will do so and you will be fine." The faith he had in my future helped me over many a rough spot. He believed that I could do it, and that did a lot for my self-confidence.

It's important that you play to the widow's strengths and hold out hope for her future. Work with her in a way that helps her see for herself that life can be good again. The day will come, as it did for me, when she will take those first wobbly steps toward a truly new life. The day came when I could cherish memories of Martin and not feel searing pain. And the day came when I could walk into a bank or lawyer's office or anyplace else and not feel that each step was bringing me closer to the brink of disaster. I needed to and eventually did accept Martin's death, but I also needed to keep part of him alive. Don't make the mistake of thinking that having memories and recalling special moments is a refusal to let go of the past. Our ability to finally laugh and to cry at the thought of great happiness or sorrow is part of reaching the state of acceptance. Don't expect the widow in your life to bury the past with her husband. She needs to accept the reality of death, and she also needs to find a place inside where love can continue to survive. My despair was with me for a long time, but at some point I found myself looking forward to tomorrow without dread. You can do a great deal to encourage a widow, and the first step is to care. The next step is to learn, to educate yourself, and the ones that follow put it into practice. My hope for the widow in your life is that you are willing to take those extra steps. The responsibility is great, but the rewards are rich. You have my gratitude for making the effort.

EPILOGUE

In 1983 I developed cancer. I had a lump in my breast that turned out to be malignant. I had a lumpectomy, was given chemotherapy, and it was OK for a while. Then I had a recurrence and another round of chemotherapy. Last checkup I was fine, but I feel something in my neck again and I'm worried. I have difficulty swallowing, and my daughter, Elizabeth, has been urging me to go to the doctor. I wanted to wait until I was due for the annual, mostly because I wanted to get my affairs in order.

As I became increasingly concerned about my health, I began to write the most dramatic of scripts. I can't swallow, therefore it must be in my throat. The doctor is going to remove my throat, or maybe I'll choke to death. It's been keeping me awake at night. Finally, Elizabeth couldn't stand it anymore and took the initiative and called her brother, Jon. She told him how worried she was about me. Jon called me and said the most extraordinary things. He said, "Don't spare me. What's going on with you? I think you ought to come to my house and talk to me." I thought that was a great thing. I welcomed the invitation. I couldn't wait to go. I've been advocating being open about death and dying for a long time, and here was my chance to put what I had learned to the test.

When I went up to see Jon it was with that purpose, but I didn't know how much he could take. We sat down together, and I showed him the papers I had filled out for donating my organs and my body to research at Columbia Presbyterian Medical Center. I felt that was a good thing to do. I knew they would dispose of my body. They would bury me or do whatever I designated, and I felt that I didn't want my children to have to cope with that. I showed him the living will I had gotten and explained that I didn't want any heroic measures. Having watched my husband die a long, agonizing death when the prognosis was zero made me feel very strongly about that.

I also told Jon that I'm not afraid to die, and I'm not. I had an experience not too long ago that made me realize something about death.

During a visit to Virginia, I was offered

the opportunity to participate in the Monroe Institute's Explorer's Program, a monitored session in the laboratory where Robert Monroe's patented Hemi-sync sound tapes are used to help the participant achieve altered states of consciousness.[*]I have practiced meditation since Martin's death, and I felt this might be an extension of my relaxed thoughts while meditating. Actually it put me in touch with feelings and messages and sights far beyond my imagination.

What it did for me was to lessen my fear of death and open up the possibility of another state of being. The most powerful impression I have of the experience is of a bodilessness, of being free of a body that has been giving me pain and anxiety. I was free of the body, but still alive. It was amazing and wonderful, and I began to think of death as the next great adventure.

I don't necessarily care about the next world, if there is a next world. I don't believe that is our task. I believe our purpose here is to celebrate the life we have—to bring

[*]Robert A. Monroe is the author of *Far Journeys* (New York: Doubleday, 1986) and *Journeys out of the Body* (New York: Dolphin, 1971–1986) and the director of the Monroe Institute in Faber, Virginia.

joy into our lives and into the lives of others. It's hard sometimes to feel joyful when cancer makes the possibility of death so real. I'm trying not to look so far ahead. I have to stay in the present, and do what I can do each day.

What was most important to me was that I was able to tell Jon and to describe to him exactly how I felt about all these things, and he didn't get crazy, he didn't freak out, he didn't get frightened. He said he was pleased that I wasn't afraid of dying. He liked the idea of death as another adventure, as I do. And he said, he would do anything he could to help me. I can't tell you how relieved I was. It took a lot of pressure off me. I stayed with him for four days and came back to New York feeling that I had confided exactly how I felt to one of the two people I'm closest to in the world, and he accepted it. I am so grateful to have the opportunity to put into practice the very things I've been talking about for nearly twenty years.

I've learned not only from my own experience, but from so many others who have not been able to explore their feelings about dying and death. The consequences for the people who love you are disastrous, and everybody is frustrated because of the unfinished business. Now that I have talked about it, I feel that I have a support system with my children and with my close friends. I feel surrounded by a golden circle of love. That makes it much easier to face what I have to face.

I was so touched by my children. Because I live with Elizabeth, it may be a little easier for me to talk to Jon. I'm too close to her. And also she's younger and had two parents for a much shorter time than Jon did. I was very careful to write her a long letter before I went up to visit Jon, thanking her for calling him and for caring. If it weren't for Elizabeth, I wouldn't have made that trip. I wouldn't have had that experience. She instigated the whole thing, and I'll always be grateful—more than she knows. I hope I'll be able to talk with her even more. I've made plenty of mistakes with my children, but the one thing that I care about very much—and they both know it—is communication. I believe communication is love. If that has gotten through to them, I will be very happy.

There are other pieces of business for me to take care of. There are financial things and living arrangements to think about and personal possessions that I want to go to various people. I've often heard how bereaved survivors fight over possessions. A woman I knew held a get-together she called Choosers, and she invited everyone who was in the will to come up and choose what they wanted while she was still alive. Then she marked each thing so there wouldn't be any problem or argument afterward. I'd like to do that. These are just some of the things I'm trying to anticipate while I still can.

Life is so fragile. Anything can happen at any time. It's something I've had to think about and something we should all think about more than we do. I may live a long while yet, but talking to my children and getting things in order have made everything easier, for them and for me.

Grief itself is hard enough to get over. The people who love you don't need any more burdens to deal with. So I've decided that whatever time is left will be spent celebrating the life I have and trying to lighten the burden of those who will grieve for me.

Lynn Caine died of cancer December 16, 1987 at Columbia Presbyterian Medical Center in New York City. Her innovative work remains an inspiration and a guiding force for widows and for many others suffering loss.

RESOURCES

ORGANIZATIONS

Alcoholics Anonymous
AA World Services
P.O. Box 459
Grand Central Station
New York, N.Y. 10017
(212) 473-6200

Self-help program for
adult alcoholics

American Association of
   Suicidology
2459 S. Ash
Denver, Col. 80222
(303) 692-0985

Self-help group referrals

Association of Retired
   Persons
Widowed Persons Service
1909 K Street, NW
Washington, D.C. 20049
(202) 872-4700

Offers many services,
including referrals to
local widow groups,
reading lists, newsletters

Battered Women Self-Help
Victims Services Agency
Two Lafayette St.
New York, N.Y. 10007
(212) 577-7700

Referrals for counseling
and self-help groups

Big Brothers/Big Sisters of America 230 N. Thirteenth Philadelphia, Pa. 19107 (215) 567-7000	National volunteer organization offering counseling and referrals throughout the country
Displaced Homemakers Network 1411 K St., NW, Suite 930 Washington, D.C. 20005 (202) 628-6767	Career counseling and job-search information
Emotions Anonymous P.O. Box 4245 St. Paul, Minn. 55104 (612) 647-9217	Self-help group referrals for persons suffering from depression or anxiety
Families of Homicide Victims Program c/o Victim Services Agency Two Lafayette Street New York, N.Y. 10007 (212) 577-7700	Offers referrals for counseling
Gray Panthers 311 S. Juniper St., Suite 601 Philadelphia, Pa. 19107 (215) 347-3403	Advocates for fundamental social change in discrimination against the aging
Growing Through Grief P.O. Box 269 Arnold, Md. 21012 (301) 974-4224	Sponsors workshops on grief process and offers referrals to support groups, speakers bureau

The League of Women Voters 1730 M St., NW Washington, D.C. 20036 (202) 347-3403	Activist network that encourages citizens to participate in government and public policy; referrals, information
National Council of Senior Citizens 925 15th St., NW Washington, D.C. 20005 (202) 347-8800	Nonprofit advocacy organization
Parents Without Partners 8807 Colesville Road Silver Spring, Md. 20910 (800) 638-8078	Support groups and social gatherings; referrals from its national office
National Hospice Organization 1901 N. Fort Myer Dr. Suite 307 Arlington, Va. 22209 (703) 243-5900	Referrals for grief counseling and hospice information
National Organization for Women 1401 New York Ave., NW, Suite 800 Washington, D.C. 20005–2102 (202) 347-2279	Many services and referrals
National Self-Help Clearing House 33 W. Forty-second St. Room 620N New York, N.Y. 10036 (212) 840-1259	Referrals for self-help groups throughout the country

Older Women's League (OWL) 730 Eleventh Street NW, Suite 300 Washington, D.C. 20001 (202) 783-6686	Referrals and information, many services
Suicide Prevention Center 184 Salem St. Dayton, Ohio 45406 (513) 223-9096	Self-help group referrals
Theos Foundation (They Help Each Other Spiritually) Penn Hills Mall Office Bldg. Suite 410 Pittsburgh, Pa. 15235 (412) 243-4200	Referrals for widow groups; has a spiritual orientation
YWCA of the USA 726 Broadway New York, N.Y. 10003 (212) 614-2700	Many services and referrals

RECOMMENDED READING

Antoniak, Helen. *Alone: Emotional, Legal and Financial Help for the Widowed or Divorced Woman.* New York: Simon and Schuster, 1986.

Barbach, Lonnie Garfield. *For Yourself: The Fulfillment of Female Sexuality*. New York: Doubleday, 1976.

Barker, Becky. *Answers*. Corpus Christi, Tex.: Answers Period, Inc., 1984.

Benson, Herbert. *The Relaxation Response*. New York: William Morrow and Co., 1975.

Bolles, Richard N. *What Color is Your Parachute? A Practical Manual for Job-hunters and Career-changers*. Berkeley, Calif: Ten Speed Press, 1988.

Cousins, Norman. *The Healing Heart*. New York: W. W. Norton and Co., 1983.

Gawain, Shakti. *Creative Visualization*. New York: Bantam Books, 1982.

Grollman, Earl. *Explaining Death to Children*. Boston: Beacon Press, 1976.

Hewitt, John H. *After Suicide*. Philadelphia: The Westminster Press, 1980.

Jewitt, Claudia L., and S. Hadley. *Helping Children Cope with Separation and Loss.* Boston: Harvard Commons Press, 1982.

Kübler-Ross, Elisabeth. *On Death and Dying.* New York: Macmillan Co., 1970.

Levine, Steven. *A Gradual Awakening.* New York: Doubleday, 1979.

——. *Who Dies?* New York: Doubleday, 1982.

N.O.W./Legal Defense and Education Fund and Dr. Renee Cherow-O'Leary. *The State-by-State Guide to Women's Legal Rights.* New York: McGraw-Hill Book Co., 1987.

Peck, M. Scott. *The Road Less Travelled: A New Psychology of Love, Traditional Values and Spiritual Growth.* New York: Simon and Schuster, 1978.

Parkes, Colin Murray. *Bereavement: Studies of Grief in Adult Life.* Madison, Conn.: International Universities Press, Inc., 1987.

INDEX

abandonment:
  children's fear of, 172, 175
  as dream theme, 139,
    142–148
abstract reasoning, of teenagers, 159
accidents:
  anger and, 56–58
  death and, 165
  insurance for, 312–313
accountants, complaints
  about, 321–322
action:
  depression and, 68
  self-confidence and, 202
adrenaline, 55, 103
adultery, 268–269
advice, giving of, 362–365
afterlife, death and, 166
aggressive behavior, 210,
  211, 220
aging, in men vs. women,
  267–268
agoraphobia, 90–91
AIDS, 244, 245, 256
alarm clocks:
  meditation and, 114
  wake-ups and, 92
Albert, Prince, 27
alcohol:
  as depressant, 127
  sex and, 269–270

see also drinking
Alcoholics Anonymous
  (AA), 107, 129, 382
Alcoholism, bereavement
  compared with, 107
alternate-nostril breathing,
  123–124
American Association of
  Retired Persons (AARP),
  334, 344, 382
American Association of
  Suicidology, 382
American Bar Association,
  316, 321
American Medical Associa-
  tion, 334
amino acids, 85
anger, 12, 47, 48–60
  accidents and, 57–58
  in aggressive behavior,
    210, 211
  assertive widows and,
    203–205
  of children, 172
  dating and, 51–53
  dreams and, 134, 135, 143
  quiet, 53
  releasing of, 53–57, 66
  unexpressed
    (inner-directed), 59, 67
animals:
  death of, 157, 163–164

390

392

wedding rings,
    throwing away of, 52, 54
Weiss, Robert, 32
"what-if?" syndrome, 106
When I Say No I Feel Guilty
    (Smith), 217
Widow (Caine), 3, 4,
    8–9, 59, 186, 243, 337
    origins of, 284–285
widowers, mortality rate for,
    7
widows, widowhood:
    assertive, *see* assertive
        widows
    average age of, 335
    descriptions of, 186–188
    as "invisible legion," 341
    mortality rate for, 7
    number of, 305
    older, 33, 227
    poverty of, 336–337
    resources for, 304–344,
        382–385
    stages of, 4–7
    see also specific topics
widows' support groups, 32,
    75, 315
    guilt and, 64, 66
Widow's Survival Checklist,
    311–314
wills, 310, 312, 332
women's organizations,
    318–320
work, *see* careers
Working with Dreams
    (Ullman), 136
writing:
    as coping mechanism,
        34–37, 109
    to elected officials,

326–331
    journals, 34–37, 134, 140
    relaxation and, 83

yoga, 85
Young Women's Christian
    Association (YWCA), 340,
    344, 385

405

The publishers hope that this
Large Print Book has brought
you pleasurable reading.
Each title is designed to make
the text as easy to see as possible.
G.K. Hall Large Print Books
are available from your library and
your local bookstore. Or, you can
receive information by mail on
upcoming and current Large Print Books
and order directly from the publishers.
Just send your name and address to:

G.K. Hall & Co.
70 Lincoln Street
Boston, Mass. 02111

or call, toll-free:

1-800-343-2806

A note on the text
Large print edition designed by
Pauline Chin.
Composed in 18 pt Plantin
on a Xyvision 300/Linotron 202N
by Tara Casey
of G.K. Hall & Co.